PLUG-AND-PLAY EDUCATION

Plug-and-Play Education: Knowledge and Learning in the Age of Platforms and Artificial Intelligence documents and critiques how the education sector is changing with the advancement of ubiquitous edtech platforms and automation. As programmability and computation reengineer institutions towards efficiency and prediction, the perpetual collection of and access to digital data is creating complex opportunities and concerns. Drawing from research into secondary and higher education settings, this book examines the influence of digital "infrastructuring", the automation of teaching and learning, and the very purpose of education in a context of growing platformisation and artificial intelligence integration. These theoretical, practical, and policy-oriented insights will offer educational technologists, designers, researchers, and policymakers a more inclusive, diverse, and open-ended perspective on the design and implementation of learning technologies.

Carlo Perrotta is Associate Professor of Digital Education in the Faculty of Education at the University of Melbourne, Australia.

PLUG-AND-PLAY EDUCATION

Knowledge and Learning in the Age of Platforms and Artificial Intelligence

Carlo Perrotta

NEW YORK AND LONDON

Designed cover image: © shutterstock

First published 2024
by Routledge
605 Third Avenue, New York, NY 10158

and by Routledge
4 Park Square, Milton Park, Abingdon, Oxon, OX14 4RN

Routledge is an imprint of the Taylor & Francis Group, an informa business

© 2024 Carlo Perrotta

The right of Carlo Perrotta to be identified as author of this work has been asserted in accordance with sections 77 and 78 of the Copyright, Designs and Patents Act 1988.

All rights reserved. No part of this book may be reprinted or reproduced or utilised in any form or by any electronic, mechanical, or other means, now known or hereafter invented, including photocopying and recording, or in any information storage or retrieval system, without permission in writing from the publishers.

Trademark notice: Product or corporate names may be trademarks or registered trademarks, and are used only for identification and explanation without intent to infringe.

Library of Congress Cataloging-in-Publication Data
Names: Perrotta, Carlo, author.
Title: Plug-and-play education : knowledge and learning
in the age of platforms and artificial intelligence / Carlo Perrotta.
Description: New York, NY : Routledge, 2024. |
Includes bibliographical references and index.
Identifiers: LCCN 2023057015 (print) | LCCN 2023057016 (ebook) |
ISBN 9780367567903 (hardback) | ISBN 9780367568917 (paperback) |
ISBN 9781003099826 (ebook)
Subjects: LCSH: Education--Effect of technological innovations on. |
Artificial intelligence--Educational applications. |
Education--Aims and objectives.
Classification: LCC LB1028.3 .P397 2024 (print) |
LCC LB1028.3 (ebook) | DDC 371.33--dc23/eng/20240123
LC record available at https://lccn.loc.gov/2023057015
LC ebook record available at https://lccn.loc.gov/2023057016

ISBN: 978-0-367-56790-3 (hbk)
ISBN: 978-0-367-56891-7 (pbk)
ISBN: 978-1-003-09982-6 (ebk)

DOI: 10.4324/9781003099826

Typeset in Times New Roman
by SPi Technologies India Pvt Ltd (Straive)

For Annabel, who gave me the time.

CONTENTS

Acknowledgements   *ix*

1 Introduction   1

Platforms and platformisation 3
Academia pays attention: The rise of platform
and infrastructure studies 7
Structure of the book 10
Note 12
References 12

2 Platformed education: Key concepts   13

Platformisation, datafication, and data infrastructures 13
The plug-and-play imaginary 14
Infrastructuring 19
Platformed participation 24
Conclusion 29
Note 31
References 31

3 Educating in platforms   34

Is platformisation a transformative moment in the
history of educational theory and practice? 34

viii Contents

*Learning science: Is platformed learning a form of
self-regulated learning? 35*
The infrastructural curriculum of platformisation 40
Platformed learning as topological dwelling 44
Conclusion 48
References 49

4 The unreasonable AI of platformisation   53

*The relationship between AI, automation,
and platformisation 53*
The seven pieces of the current AI jigsaw 55
The unreasonableness of AI 57
Unreasonable AI and educational responsibility 62
Interpreting unreasonable AI 64
The automation of education: The big picture 66
Conclusion 69
References 71

5 Understanding platforms: Towards a social epistemology   74

The concept of understanding 74
Platformisation as episteme 76
The platformed episteme and educational understanding 80
Conclusion 85
References 85

6 Some notes on the empirical study of platformisation
   and automation in education   88

Control 88
Modelling 90
Topology 97
Conclusion 100
References 102

7 Conclusion   105

A final remark 111
Note 113
References 113

Index   *115*

ACKNOWLEDGEMENTS

The idea for this book originated in 2018. It morphed into an actual project in 2020, only to be held back by the disruption caused by the global pandemic – and by some unrelated health issues not worth getting into. As it is often the case with these monographs, the final output is as much the culmination of a subjective research programme as the result of multiple exchanges with colleagues and friends. This is just a partial list. Neil Selwyn comes first, as a generous mentor who was there at two key junctures of my research journey into education technology – around the very start and after a long period of post-doctoral meandering across UK academia, which eventually led me to the lontanissima Australia. Another amazing critical edtech researcher I had the luck to share mind-space with is Ben Williamson. Ben and I also go back a long way – to the heady days of Bristol's Futurelab to be precise, where it all began for me. Each time our paths crossed I walked away a better scholar. Mathias Decuypere has recently been a source of innovative thinking. He read a chapter and provided immensely helpful feedback. Others who inspired me to think more deeply and theoretically around the issues covered in this book are Kalervo Gulson, Luci Pangrazio, Janja Komljenovic, Sam Sellar, Jessica Holloway, Steve Lewis, Scott Bulfin, Dragan Gasevic, Michael Henderson, Jason Beech, Sigrid Hartong, and more who will hopefully forgive me for not having them included.

Finally, thanks to my Editor Daniel Schwartz for the extensions, the advice, and, more generally, for being a very decent and kind person.

1

INTRODUCTION

> It's a peculiar apparatus.
> Franz Kafka, In the Penal Colony

I started working on this book at the beginning of 2020, with the optimistic idea of writing a straightforward monograph about the growing role of platforms in education. During that eventful and, for many, tragic year, it became clear that while this topic was already important before the pandemic, its significance had exploded and acquired a more complex set of connotations. For most people working in education, as well as millions of households around the world, 2020 will be remembered as the year of mass school closures followed by the "Great Online Pivot", when entire education systems rapidly, and often haphazardly, transitioned to distance education. The breathless expansion of the educational technology industry, already a topic of scrutiny for many critically minded researchers and commentators, became a matter of pressing public interest.

The most puzzling, and in hindsight paralysing, development during the initial frantic months of 2020 was an implicit, and forceful, narrative of eagerness and helpfulness, fuelled by the drama unfolding before our very eyes. It was no longer a time to be critical academics, but to roll up sleeves and deliver online learning resources to panic-stricken educators around the world; or, if unable to do so, to use our limited ideation skills to re-imagine the purpose of education in a nebulous post-pandemic world. Meanwhile, digital platforms were making strides in education, tightening their grip in areas – from policy to pedagogy – they had already colonised through data-based efficiencies and the tantalising promise of predictive personalisation.

DOI: 10.4324/9781003099826-1

2 Introduction

The explosion of generative AI in 2022 was another disruptive event for education, the world writ large, and more modestly for the scholarly project that animates this book. It became soon clear that we are racing towards a scenario where various flavours of AI are fully and invisibly integrated into existing platform "ecosystems",[1] enabling the easy outsourcing of a growing list of tasks and responsibilities. As I write this introduction, AI models like Generative Pre-trained Transformer (GPT) seem poised to become structural and unavoidable components of our digitally mediated interactions: searching the web, creating content, accessing and using essential services, consuming entertainment and, last but not least, engaging in formal or informal learning.

Following these tumultuous years, the book needed to change its course and embrace a stronger emphasis on theoretical analysis to address the existential anxiety that emerged in education around the role of platforms and AI. It became also clear that such an analysis needed to challenge the mainstream narrative of evidence-based education if it was to say anything meaningful. On the one hand, there is sufficient evidence that the automated logics of platforms and AI enable efficiency and personalisation, helping educators reach out to underserved students, and tailoring the learning experience around diverse needs and motivations. On the other hand, these benefits come at a cost, which can be pithily described as the tyranny of scale: a seemingly contradictory alliance of reductionism and magnitude, where simple behaviours selected not for their salience but for their enumerability can be controlled through totalising and ever-increasing forms of surveillance. The conceptual distinction between the well-documented benefits of data-based educational technologies and the social and epistemological price we are asked to pay for them is a good initial step for a deep dive into platformisation in education. It sets the tone for the book and provides a segue into the first introductory discussion aimed at clearing the definitional ground.

Before we begin, a clarification about the title and the scope of the book is needed. The principle of plug-and-play has become a ubiquitous metaphor for our relationship with technology and is a manifestation of the power vested in those who design and maintain digital infrastructures. This deceptively simple concept carries profound implications, embodying a deliberate choice of obliviousness to the intricate workings that lie beneath the surface. In a world where the complexity of technological systems is beyond the comprehension of the average individual, the act of plugging in a device and expecting it to work hinges on an implicit trust in the infrastructure, with users willingly embracing a form of ignorance about what happens "under the hood". Jacques Derrida's notion of the archive as a repository of knowledge and power is relevant here. The intricacies of technology are archived, hidden from plain view, and accessible only to those with specialised expertise. Users, in an act of deliberate obliviousness, relinquish agency over this hidden archive, ceding control to infrastructure providers and administrators.

> [T]here is no political power without control of the archive, if not memory. Effective democratization can always be measured by this essential criterion: the participation in and access to the archive, its constitution, and its interpretation.
>
> *(Derrida, 1996, p. 11)*

Therefore, the plug-and-play principle serves as a metaphorical lens through which we can examine the dynamics of platformisation, where trust and the relinquishing of understanding are not accidental but are integral to the exercise of power in the digital age. Against this backdrop, the book offers a subjective synthesis of a programme of scholarship around platformisation and AI in education. It stands on the shoulders of others – colleagues and friends who have written extensively about educational technology from a critical sociological perspective, and who will be duly acknowledged in the individual chapters. In this sense, the book's aspiration is to represent and celebrate the achievement of a stage of relative maturity in the field of "platform studies in education", which, of course, calls for a degree of theoretical and methodological formalisation. Mindful of this aspiration, the book takes a broad view of education without committing to one sector, although most points will apply to secondary and tertiary education, with a particular focus on broadly comparable English-speaking contexts such as the United States, the UK, and Australia. Although there are a great many differences between secondary and post-secondary education, it could be argued that several overarching sociotechnical dynamics and enduring contradictions are shared. These include teaching and learning under conditions of growing digitisation, the nature of knowledge and understanding in platformed contexts, and the empirical study of platformisation and automation in education.

The book strives to remain accessible in language, but it does engage with theory at several levels; hence, reading can be enhanced by an entry-level familiarity with certain disciplines and areas of scholarship: sociology, psychology, computer science, and Science and Technology Studies (STS). In addition to researchers, I am confident that those with a strategic and "political" interest in education will find the book helpful. Conversely, I fear that readers seeking readily applicable evidence to inform classroom practice may find it underwhelming. I encourage them to stick around nonetheless, as they may find most arguments to have important, if indirect, practical implications.

Platforms and platformisation

In layman terms, digital platforms are networked software environments that offer disparate services and affordances. They operate by mediating

4 Introduction

between the supply and demand of services, or between people seeking informal sociality and entertainment. While broadly accurate and easy to grasp, this definition is clearly insufficient, as it encompasses very diverse enterprises operating in different contexts: social media platforms like Facebook and Twitter, content creation platforms like YouTube, ride-share platforms like Uber, and, of course, explicitly educational platforms like Khan Academy, Coursera, and Google Classroom. As it is often the case, economic models help create helpful categories that can be used across sectors. These models are not mutually exclusive, and they often coexist. Nonetheless, they help us draw some broad outlines within which we can locate our elusive object of analysis. They are as follows:

I.   Multisided markets. A multisided market can be broadly defined as a transactional arrangement where groups of self-interested users provide benefits to each other across a network, following a "win-win" principle where suppliers, intrinsically inclined to offer a particular service, and customers, intrinsically motivated to access that service, can connect smoothly. As the network grows, all parties have more chances to turn a profit. These are the "network effects" that all digital platforms pursue.

II. Taking a cut: the platform captures a fraction of the value generated in the transactions between providers and seekers of a service, for instance in the context of multisided transactions.

III. Loss leading: a valuable service (e.g., a well-designed webmail service like Gmail) is offered for free, which leads to universal adoption of other services or functionalities that belong to a broader, proprietary platform ecosystem. Tailored "premium" functionalities are then developed and sold.

IV. Monetising data: personal data are captured through algorithmic surveillance and sold for marketing purposes, which in most cases means personalised advertising.

V.   Rentiership: the platform seeks control over "assets", understood as any resource that holds value by virtue of its potential to generate future revenues: user data, collective knowledge, analytical capabilities, storage, and so forth. This leads to a situation where the platform extracts profits (rents) by leveraging intellectual property rights or monopolistic dominance.

VI. Philanthropy: the platform relies entirely or partly on private donations – often from wealthy organisations or individuals who play prominent roles in the technology sector.

While offering a fairly accurate synoptic overview of the economic landscape, these six models are only partially effective towards a definition which has educational relevance, and while the economic dimension is crucial to develop an understanding of any platform, no matter the sector in which it operates, it is not the only lens. Perhaps, the attempt to build taxonomies is inherently flawed, doomed to be a never-ending process of revision, expansion, and, of course, arbitration. For this reason, this book is not much about typologies of educational platforms but "platformisation", understood as a broad set of logics concerned with the re-organisation of social life through and around digitisation, prediction, and automation. This clarification is therefore the main point of departure, and it informs the conceptual framework that underpins the chapters that will follow. Expanding upon this initial clarification, the book also understands platformisation as a process of institutional mimesis – a view that draws on Vallas and Schor's perceptive analysis where platforms are described as "chameleons whose effects are contingent on the institutional environments within which they operate" (Vallas & Schor, 2020, p. 281). For instance, the contested global growth of Uber during the late 2010s was partly shaped by the regulatory structures of the national contexts where the company sought to penetrate. In the United States, given the unregulated nature of the labour market, Uber became mostly associated with employment insecurity. In Europe, the rapid advance of ride-share apps generated a slightly different political debate about democratic control over urban transportation, as well as issues of taxation.

As Vallas and Schor noted, platforms' propensity to mould themselves around local regulatory legislation proves that they are not mere instruments of extraction and exploitation but can be used to enhance participation for underrepresented groups; indeed, the same technologies used to control and exploit can be repurposed to offer safeguards and more effective governance of common resources and infrastructure. At the same time, the institutional mimesis enacted through platformisation is not an entirely neutral affair, but it comes with significant strings attached. We must therefore problematise the mimetic plasticity of platforms as a phenomenon beholden to capitalist notions of value capture. For platformisation to occur, there must be preexisting social or economic orderings which, over time, have developed contractual conventions, bureaucratic structures, and tacit rituals. These orderings reproduce the social world as we know it, but historically their contractual and ritualistic over-complexity placed limits on capitalistic value appropriation (Han, 2020). Ethical-political arrangements developed over time for governance purposes, with gatekeepers, intermediaries, guarantors, legal protocols, and so forth. Platformisation uses digital technology to mimic and then reshape these arrangements, configuring the platform as the only regulating mechanism governing a pre-existing network of value, and remediating the relationships between people and resources. This process

6 Introduction

involves the creation of datafied and adaptive affordances that grant faster, cheaper, more transactional, more automated, and fully on-demand access to something which was already valuable before. Just plug it in and play it.

In the context of platformed conviviality, this adaptive, plug-and-play logic relies on the natural drives of humans – to socialise and mingle in various ways – but does away with the ritualised and emotionally demanding dimension of many face-to-face situations. The best example in this case is perhaps online dating platforms, followed closely by the way in which the basic conventions of reasoned discourse are "streamlined" or downright suspended on platforms like Twitter (or "X" as it came to be known in 2023) or Facebook. In a more conventional economic context – for example, the service sector – platformisation relies on human labour and communal assets (skills, infrastructure, private property, and local knowledge) but does away with forms of contractual governance and the associated safeguards for workers and clients. The perfect example is again ride-sharing platforms that rely on the private ownership of vehicles, the will and ability to drive them, and well-maintained urban infrastructure funded through public taxation. This is indeed the "rentiership" model mentioned earlier, where platform owners earn economic returns (rents) by imposing a form of monopolistic and datafied control over valuable resources often produced and maintained by society (Sadowski, 2020). In the context of education, which is the focus here, platformisation follows similar templates, but it cannot be neatly reduced to a single instance of "value capture" like in the previous examples.

Indeed, the complexity of this field compared to other spheres warrants an extraordinary descriptive effort. Education is many things at the same time: a structured system for knowledge transmission and creation, a childcare institution historically associated with women's ability to participate in the economy, a set of long-term policies that indirectly impact on a country's economic performance, and a path to self-realisation and informed citizenship. Moreover, national differences still matter in education, perhaps more so than in other areas. There are many distinct educational microcosms around the world where global trends must align with local politics and cultures. The overarching mimetic logic outlined before, however, does not change. Platformisation in education operates by colonising and then appropriating pre-existing value-generating arrangements, with instances of platformisation that impact on the pedagogical dimensions, and instances that impact on other cultural and socially reproductive functions. Platform logics, in other words, certainly target teaching and learning but also parental engagement, relationships between the education system and the private sector, the function of schooling as a temporary enclosure for young people, the dynamics of knowledge creation and dissemination (publishing) in the tertiary sector, and so forth. For any explicit or implicit facet of education, there is (or there will soon be) an app, a benchmarking platform, a multi-sided communication tool, a dynamic database and countless application programming interfaces (APIs) that enable interactions between data, developers and users. It is important to emphasise once more that platform logics are introduced ex post and superimposed, often in highly contingent ways and even haphazardly, on something that was already there, which suggests that platformisation is not much about innovation or disruption, but about co-existing with and reconfiguring the status quo following principles of economic rationality: choice, efficiency, predictive control, and maximum benefit at a reduced cost.

Moreover, this economic rationality is entangled with the distinctive techno-centric cultures that originated in English-speaking countries over the past half-century, and it manifests materially as a planetary network of proprietary infrastructures mostly controlled by a monopoly of US technology companies. Schools and universities around the world – from the global north to the global south – can plug into these proprietary global infrastructures to outsource management and administrative functions, while teachers and learners have access to cloud-hosted suites of digital tools powered by adaptive learning analytics. The magnitude of these developments is plain to see in the everyday lives of educators and learners, and indeed they have been at the centre of much research and debate. The next section will summarise some of the more influential contributions which have informed the book. I will, of course, return to many of these ideas and themes throughout the volume.

Academia pays attention: The rise of platform and infrastructure studies

Approximately in the 2010s the term "platform" became a pliable descriptor applicable to multiple units of analysis: game console systems (Montfort & Bogost, 2009), proprietary software environments (e.g., Microsoft and Apple), and social media and content-sharing applications like Facebook and YouTube. As noted by Gillespie (2010), such vagueness and semantic flexibility were largely by design, as it enabled interested actors (developers, investors, and owners) to construct an appealing and marketable narrative of openness, adaptivity, and neutrality that deliberately obfuscated the more problematic dimensions. More recently, Poell, Nieborg, and van Dijck (2019) offered an excellent definition of platformisation: "the penetration of the infrastructures, economic processes and governmental frameworks of digital platforms in different economic sectors and spheres of life, as well as the reorganisation of cultural practices and imaginations around these platforms" (2019, p. 1). This penetration has been largely spearheaded by a small group of technology giants, who have shaped the platformisation paradigm around a handful of infrastructural "first principles": surveillance, automation, interoperability, and value extraction at scale. To claim that these principles are "infrastructural" means that alongside the production of material arrangements designed to collect, store, process and transform data, there are ontological aspects involved, which create specific "ways of being in the world" (Larkin, 2013, p. 330). This is, after all, what all infrastructures tend to do: they provide a framework for life as we know it by regulating flows of resources, information, and people, and by providing communicative scripts for social interactions. The entire phenomenology of modern life can be described as a collection of enactments and relationships mediated by infrastructures – from urban transportation to the internet. As a result, the interface between the social study of infrastructures and platform studies emerged recently as a fertile area of scholarship, which is beginning to illuminate the ways in which "platformed infrastructures" are overlaid on top of public infrastructures owned by sovereign states (Plantin et al., 2018). Indeed, we are rapidly reaching a point where public institutions have become so dependent on proprietary digital infrastructures for all their datafied management needs that it is difficult to imagine how they could be disentangled without entire societies grinding to a halt. From a historical perspective, it seems obvious that education was going to become a significant arena for the establishment of such infrastructural dominance.

The modernist vision of mass education that emerged in the 19th century required dedicated infrastructural arrangements: classrooms designed to ensure surveillance and crowd control, curriculum and assessment standards that engendered uniformity, and enforceable disciplinary protocols that produced compliance. Digital platforms superimpose their proprietary systems and logics on top of these pre-existing arrangements, seeking to augment, rationalise, and streamline the status quo: apps and suites designed around curricular requirements (e.g., maths and literacy), learning management systems (LMSs) aligned with the administrative and organisational structures of schools and universities, social control platforms to survey attendance and behaviour (e.g., Manolev et al., 2020), and centralised data repositories hosting and analysing assessment and sociodemographic data. Platformisation, it bears repeating and possibly to the chagrin of many technology enthusiasts, is not a transformative or disruptive force in education or elsewhere. Rather, it should be viewed as the act of placing a software layer over pre-existing infrastructures. Once settled, this layer begins to extend downwards to more and more functions, and outwards to other software ecosystems. Even the notion of datafication – "the collection of data at all levels" (Jarke & Breiter, 2019, p. 1) which powers the predictions and classifications of every platforms and AI model in existence – should be conceptualised in education as the superimposition of a (private) software layer on a pre-existing apparatus of governance by numbers, which emerged after decades of managerial accountability, standardisation, and quantitative assessment (Ball, 2018; Gorur, 2017). The rationale for this superimposition is eminently political-economic: to create osmosis between the public and private sectors, incentivising the reform of education systems along neoliberal lines and reconstructing governing relations around access to and control over data.

The materialisation of this logic in practice is still a work in progress, but its ultimate goals are clear: the fragmentation and the "repackaging" of education as a collection of datafied transactions, where supply and demand can integrate seamlessly and across geographical and cultural borders. This reconfiguration can be observed in the historical trajectory of the educational technology industry. Early forms of e-learning such as the static LMSs of the mid-1990s were designed to support instruction through well-defined digital affordances: connectivity and communication, 24/7 access to course materials, time-saving and labour-saving features, and so on. Technological innovation in this space then followed the same pattern that emerged in the wake of the dotcom bust of the late 1990s, that is, during the transition from a static internet of webpages to the so-called Web 2.0. Tim O'Reilly – founder of O'Reilly Media and eminent tech guru – famously described the Web 2.0 as a new form of dynamic internet where the ability to handle large amounts of data was set to become crucially important. O'Reilly also predicted that in this new dynamic internet regular people were poised to "add value" as participants rather than as mere users, as they could now leverage their own data, enriching their personal lives and creating opportunities for themselves and commercial organisations (O'Reilly, 2005). Educational technology companies found themselves being swept away by this fast-unfolding datafication of the internet, and, as the Web 2.0 descended rapidly into "surveillance capitalism" (Zuboff, 2019), they began to embrace interoperability, scale, and analytics as paths to further innovation and growth. This transformation was accompanied by the diversification of the edtech landscape with multiple products and services – adaptive tutors, mobile apps, and MOOCs – which, despite having different purposes and sector-level use scenarios (primary, secondary, and tertiary), all reflect the growing importance of shared cloud architectures and a functional dependency on data analysis at scale. This process was aided by a growing body of academic scholarship about technology-enhanced learning, which began to coalesce around "Learning Analytics" in the 2010s and, more recently, around Artificial Intelligence in Education (AIED). Nowadays, the data collected by these edtech products and services include traditional grades and other assessment metrics, but also log-in data, resource usage data, online activities completion data, participation in forums, clicks, and trail data produced as an offshoot of other digitally mediated interactions.

This was, in other words, a case of "convergence", with the educational technology industry and research nexus gravitating towards data-based features and affordances that resemble those found in social media platforms and in the business intelligence sector. As a result, the centre of attention shifted from discrete apps, tools, and interfaces to the underlying digital infrastructures that enable interoperability between software systems, and multiple datafied interactions between a range of actors. Some of these are, of course, educators and learners – the "end users" – but the edtech landscape has been colonised by other powerful entities and parties: cloud service providers, advertisers, software developers, and armies of intermediaries and consultants. Household "Big Tech" names like Google, Microsoft, and Amazon have fuelled and coordinated this convergence by seeking to monopolise ever-larger regions of the underlying infrastructure. Microsoft was arguably the bellwether owing to its long-running leadership in the productivity software market, which propelled the personal computer into universities and schools in the 1980s and 1990s. Similarly, starting from a position of strength that matured steadily during the 2000s, Google saw its education business grow exponentially – a veritable boom that allowed the Silicon Valley giant to extend its reach into all aspects of the educational process. Amazon, on the other hand, makes large profits by selling pay-as-you-go access to networking, storage, and analytic features. Its subsidiary Amazon Web Services (AWS) is, in fact, the market leader of the cloud-based model that represents the infrastructural backbone of platformisation, vying with the other two main players (Microsoft Azure and Google Cloud) to achieve architectural dominance over the internet. In education, this translates into a large and growing market with established economic actors, nimble start-ups, schools, and universities – all of them "transacting" within specific segments (remote tutoring, e-assessment, personalised provision, etc.), while sharing the same infrastructural substrate controlled by the Amazon, Microsoft, and Google triad. This process of convergence represents the historical and technological background of the book.

Structure of the book

Following this introductory chapter, Chapter 2 will develop a preliminary conceptual discussion, following the assumption that platformisation is the result of three entwined influences. The first influence is a vision of technology as a path to human augmentation and value creation. The second influence is the role of "data infrastructuring", that is, the development of interfaces, templates, and functionalities that not only allow databases and software environments to interact with each other, but also set the conditions of access that users must comply with. A key element in this process is the progressive invisibility of digital infrastructures, leading to a sort of "algorithmic fabulation" which arises when something that has been deliberately made invisible (like a magic trick) turns into a strategy of control, underpinned by narrative of compelling and almost superhuman capabilities. The third influence is participation, framed as an ambiguous notion that reflects a tension between platform logics pursuing "user engagement", and established forms of educational participation involving teachers, students, administrators, parents, and governing bodies.

Chapter 3 stems from an acknowledgement that critical researchers of education and technology have so far neglected mainstream educational concerns, such as the nature of learning and the curriculum, in favour of sociological analyses of policy, systems, cultures, and political economies. The chapter attempts to address this limitation by asking the following question: does platformisation represent a novel approach to foster learning and to support the institutional function of education?

Chapter 4 engages with artificial intelligence, framed as the key operational component of platformisation, seamlessly integrated into infrastructures and interfaces. The chapter's driving contention is that the entire edifice of platformed AI and automation is built on the unwarranted tenet that near-total entanglement with extractive platforms is a "reasonable" proxy of educational agency.

The theoretical analysis reaches a sort of culmination in Chapter 5, where platformisation is examined as a form of "social epistemology". In particular, the chapter considers the ramifications of a key educational question: is platformisation changing our ability to understand?

Chapter 6 continues the conceptual analysis of platformisation as a form of governance, but with a more applied focus on the methodological implications. The assumption is that some engagement with methodology provides a more focused insight into a phenomenon, even if empirical research is not the goal. Nonetheless, those interested in the critical study of platformisation in education may find some helpful guidance here.

The conclusion provides a summary of the main arguments and considers more ethical and meaningful alternatives to platformisation. Here, I imagine a scenario of decentralised educational provision, and I speculate on its potential as a model for a more progressive form of education governance.

Note

1 The word "ecosystem" is used here to describe an interconnected network of individual platforms, businesses, developers, users, and institutions, which interact within a shared digital infrastructure. A notable example of platform ecosystem is Amazon Web Services (AWS), where a multitude of interconnected services and entities "interoperate".

References

Ball, S. J. (2018). *Governing by numbers: Education, governance, and the tyranny of numbers*. Routledge.

Derrida, J. (1996). *Archive fever: A Freudian impression*. University of Chicago Press.

Gillespie, T. (2010). The politics of 'platforms'. *New Media & Society, 12*, 347–364. https://doi.org/10.1177/1461444809342738

Gorur, R. (2017). Statistics and statecraft: Exploring the potentials, politics and practices of international educational assessment. *Critical Studies in Education, 58*(3), 261–265. https://doi.org/10.1080/17508487.2017.1353271

Han, B.-C. (2020). *The disappearance of rituals: A topology of the present*. Wiley.

Jarke, J., & Breiter, A. (2019). Editorial: The datafication of education. *Learning, Media and Technology, 44*(1), 1–6. https://doi.org/10.1080/17439884.2019.1573833

Larkin, B. (2013). The politics and poetics of infrastructure. *Annual Review of Anthropology, 42*(1), 327–343. https://doi.org/10.1146/annurev-anthro-092412-155522

Manolev, J., Sullivan, A., & Slee, R. (2020). The datafication of discipline: ClassDojo, surveillance and a performative classroom culture. In Jarke, J., & Breiter, A. (Eds.) *The datafication of education* (1st ed., pp. 37–52). Routledge. https://doi.org/10.4324/9780429341359

Montfort, N., & Bogost, I. (2009). *Racing the beam: The Atari video computer system*. Mit Press.

O'Reilly, T. (2005). *What Is Web 2.0 – design patterns and business models for the next generation of software*. Retrieved August, 8 2023 from https://www.oreilly.com/pub/a//web2/archive/what-is-web-20.html

Plantin, J.-C., Lagoze, C., Edwards, P. N., & Sandvig, C. (2018). Infrastructure studies meet platform studies in the age of Google and Facebook. *New Media & Society, 20*(1), 293–310. https://doi.org/10.1177/1461444816661553

Poell, T., Nieborg, D., & van Dijck, J. (2019). Platformisation. *Internet Policy Review, 8*(4). https://doi.org/10.14763/2019.4.1425

Sadowski, J. (2020). The internet of landlords: digital platforms and new mechanisms of rentier capitalism. *Antipode, 52*(2), 562–580. https://doi.org/10.1111/anti.12595

Vallas, S., & Schor, J. B. (2020). What do platforms do? Understanding the gig economy. *Annual Review of Sociology, 46*(1), 273–294. https://doi.org/10.1146/annurev-soc-121919-054857

Zuboff, S. (2019). *The age of surveillance capitalism: The fight for a human future at the new frontier of power*. Profile Books.

2

PLATFORMED EDUCATION

Key concepts

Platformisation, datafication, and data infrastructures

Platformisation is not a neatly bounded concept easily distinguishable from other ideas, most notably those of datafication and data infrastructure. There is a relative consensus in the social-scientific literature that these three notions – platformisation, datafication and data infrastructures – are profoundly related, even though they may require different methodological and analytical choices to be studied effectively. As the previous chapter began to outline, platformisation can be viewed as something operating at a higher level of theoretical abstraction. Platformisation is "what" has been happening in multiple institutional and social arenas – including education – as relations between actors are reconfigured according to the plug-and-play logics of digitisation, standardisation, efficiency, surveillance, and automation. Datafication and the development of data infrastructures could be viewed as the "how" of platformisation: they are the enabling dynamics that underpin platformisation. I follow Holloway and Lewis here who provide a definition that brings together data infrastructures and datafication in education, framing them as the combined result of "sociotechnical assemblages (i.e., people and computing hardware/software) that laboriously translate human activity into data, which are then able to be collected, stored, visualised and mediated between otherwise disparate, diverse and disconnected actors and spaces (e.g. schools, districts, states, systems)" (Holloway & Lewis, 2022, p. 4).

In practice, this laborious translation entails the creation of "standards-based technical-economic systems" (Bratton, 2015, p. 141) that involve data

DOI: 10.4324/9781003099826-2

14 Platformed education

centres and servers, networking and communication protocols, data lakes (storage repositories for large volumes of raw and unstructured data), cloud computing services, metadata management systems, specialised professions and the associated forms of expertise, regulatory bodies, and so forth. The material and political variance of these "platformed infrastructures" is key, as they manifest in different technological forms and may bring about contradictory social enactments. For instance, data infrastructures operate in education at a systemic level through the implementation of state or district-level interoperability systems (Gulson & Sellar, 2019). However, these broad systems often belie expansive and disordered local circumstances, characterised by idiosyncratic approaches to data collection and analysis, with infrastructures locked in a state of constant precariousness and upkeep where multiple actors must work behind the scenes to ensure relative standards of functionality. Against this complex background, the attempt to draw a coherent conceptual picture applicable to platformisation, datafication, and data infrastructures is not an easy task but is one worth undertaking. The result is a tentative framework based on the combined influence of three elements which have been analysed extensively in the scholarly discourse:

A) Imagined futures of digital transformation and empowerment, shared across several areas of human activity and expression: literature, politics and even religion. In the context of platformisation, these imagined futures have a foundational purpose: they create promissory narratives of future gains (material and immaterial) that catalyse public attention and economic interest.
B) Material and symbolic infrastructuring – where the use of a verb implies a dynamic and fluid process (a "doing") rather than the development of unitary and self-contained technological systems (Hartong & Piattoeva, 2021).
C) A specific form of participation, that is, a distinctive way through which people share spaces, times and practices within and across fully or partially digitised contexts.

These three concepts will be explained in the remainder of this chapter, examining their broader theoretical relevance as well as their educational implications.

The plug-and-play imaginary

Stanislaw Lem is considered one of the most successful science fiction writers outside of the English-speaking world. Born in Lwów, Poland (now Lviv, Ukraine), Lem's magnum opus is the *Cyberiad*, first published in English in 1974. The book is a collection of short stories often featuring the interstellar adventures of Trurl and Klapaucious, cosmic constructors "who could kindle or extinguish suns as easily as shelling peas" (Lem, 2014, p. 31). The two characters are sympathetic and parodic embodiments of the fixations, ambitions, and pettiness of engineering and scientific mindsets. During their "first sally" into space, Trurl and Klapaucious land on a small planet with only one continent and two warring kingdoms. After a brief counsel, the two decide to test the never-before attempted Gargantius effect on the unsuspecting inhabitants. They part ways, and each offers his services to one of the two kingdoms. Predictably, the two warring rulers (Atrocitus and Ferocitus) require the development of deadly weaponry. Thus, the two constructors separately enact Gargantius' scheme by connecting individuals into a unified, matrix-style network greatly augmenting their military capacity:

> Into each recruit (...) a plug is screwed in front, a socket in back. Upon the command Close up those ranks! the plugs and sockets connect and, where only before you had a crowd of civilians, there stands a battalion of perfect soldiers.
>
> *(38)*

However, the increased efficiency of the networking process and the subsequent emergence of a shared consciousness rapidly led to "navel contemplation" among the linked-up individuals. This is, to the reader's surprise, the actual effect that Gargantius had theorised. The process culminates into an all-encompassing artificial harmony where all antagonisms are nullified, as "both armies went off hand in hand, picking flowers beneath the fluffy white clouds, on the field of the battle that never was" (42).

The first sally of Trurl and Klapaucious is a witty satire offering a glimpse into a vision of human interdependence and augmentation via technological means. The mischievous space engineers are the omnipotent protagonists who trick the dim-witted kings and, through superior scientific knowledge, upend their warring plans by turning opposing armies into a peaceful, interlinked collective of self-absorbed, dopey minds. Lem's fable pokes fun at dumb militarism and offers a tongue-in-cheek celebration of social engineering. As good science fiction is often prone to do, it also gives an insight into a fantasy that has been with us, adapting and occasionally changing skin, for a long time: a view of the world as amenable to technical modification and mechanical harmonisation, where engineers should be given the authority and a public mandate to use their craft for the betterment of society. The origins of this worldview can be traced back to the early 1920s, when a group of American reformists who dubbed themselves "technocrats" advocated for the "the rule of the people made effective through the agency

16 Platformed education

of their servants, the scientists and engineers" (Jones, 1990, p. 214). After the dramatic events of the Great Depression, technocrats flaunted the idea of an actual "revolt of the engineers", to replace the failing leadership of industrialists and elected politicians with the efficiency and, to use a more contemporary term, the solutionism (Morozov, 2013) enabled by technical expertise. This worldview has also been explained by David Noble as an evangelical reliance on the "technological sublime", a warped notion of technology as a transcendental force that will allow humanity's ultimate salvation from all ills (Noble, 1999). A thin red line connects the cosmic sallies of Trurl and Klapaucious, the technological sublime of the technocratic "revolutionaries" and the – perhaps reductively termed – Silicon Valley imaginary of the present time.

There is certainly more to the current sociotechnical moment than a geographically localised set of values and myths, but it makes sense to associate our contemporary technological "fixations" (Sims, 2017) with the place where some of the most powerful private companies ever existed rose to prominence in a relatively short time, commanding an unprecedented global reach and amassing grotesque amounts of wealth. The influence of this imaginary in multiple social and economic spheres has been examined extensively by academics as well as informed commentators. It has been associated with the move-fast/break-things style of innovation that permeates the tech start-up culture and, by extension, the dominant techno-economic discourse of the past two decades. It has been analysed as a utopian policy rhetoric that idolises technology whilst barely hiding how it perpetuates the well-known problems of late-stage capitalism: inequality, monopolistic tendencies, consumeristic excess, and rampant environmental degradation.

Platformed imaginaries and value creation

According to the Science and Technology Studies (STS) scholar Sheila Jasanoff, societies construct relationships between technology, science, and the political order around imagined futures. There are several possible futures, but only some are successful and are accorded a dominant position (Jasanoff & Kim, 2015). Over the course of approximately 20 years – since the rise of "big data" and the internet of platforms in the early 2000s – these dominant futures have steadily converged around the opportunities of data collection and artificial intelligence, informing three broad promissory narratives (Williamson, 2017):

a) A narrative of prediction, tied to the notion that data-driven algorithms can anticipate trends and occurrences before they happen, thereby enhancing efficiency and effectiveness.

b) A narrative of total knowledge, which entails tracking an unprecedented number of actions and behaviours across multiple contexts, leading to a future where human and societal dynamics that were once intangible and unknowable can be captured and analysed.

c) A narrative of automation, which assumes that training AI models with massive volumes of data will lead to efficiencies, augmentations and eventually to the democratisation of expertise, with people able to succeed in many complex tasks, provided they have access to the appropriate analytical and generative infrastructures.

These promissory narratives keep extending and spilling over from one area to another (cultural consumption, health, democratic governance, and of course education), progressing towards the "ever disappearing horizon that analytics infrastructures and practices pursue" (Beer, 2018, p. 15). While they certainly belong to the realm of imagination, they are grounded in real affordances and potentials. In this sense, sociotechnical imaginaries and their promissory narratives could be said to "occupy a hybrid zone between the mental and the material" (Jasanoff & Kim, 2015, p. 329), informing a cultural disposition that generates a great deal of creativity and, yes, actual innovation, but also "privileges disruption over sustainability, sharing economies over union labor, personalized access over public health, data over meaning, and security over freedom" (Levina & Hasinoff, 2017, p. 491). Historical and cultural explanations are therefore eschewed in favour of technical solutions, which are appealing because they offer a simplified account of phenomena, and an easy way out of the contractual and ritualistic tangle of lived experience.

It is important to emphasise that these promises and imaginaries drive capitalism as we know it. They capture flows of desire associated with traditional cultural structures or tropes – humanity has long fantasised about predicting the future – to "reterritorialise" them (Deleuze & Guattari, 1988) in ways that serve the needs of the economy. Promises are, for example, fundamental to enable the financialisation of companies, because they are heavily implicated in the dynamics of valuation. Accounting research has long established that economic performance is not necessarily conducive to bankruptcy and indeed it can correlate with a high financial valuation (Darrough & Ye, 2007). This became abundantly clear during the late 1990s dotcom bubble, but it is still very much the case in 2023. High valuation in the face of poor revenue is a staple of the current start-up investment paradigm, where companies' success is entirely based on imagined future gains resulting from assets, such as intellectual property, R&D capabilities and, of course, access to user data.

It is safe to say that an interest in sociotechnical imaginaries and their associated promises marked the beginning of an important research strand in the critical study of digital data and platforms in education. The focus was initially on the vagaries of education policy, where datafication and prediction became rapidly associated with a rationality that struggles to contemplate collinearity, complexity, and historicity, to privilege instead "calculable representations of preferred courses of action"(Gulson & Webb, 2017, p. 18). The nebulous and networked world of policy, however, has a historical and well-documented tendency to "motivate excursions into the material world" (Williamson, 2017, p. 43), leading to a condition where very real institutional processes are reshaped so that they can conform to promissory visions of the future. More recently, this interest evolved into a more focused effort to understand how imagined futures become part of investment strategies in education technology, where "futuring" operates as a full-fledged social practice of financial valuation (Williamson & Komljenovic, 2023). This reflects an important shift in the study of platformisation as a broad economic paradigm. While initial theorisations examined the transition in the purpose of data extraction from a way to improve services to a way to collect advertising revenues (Srnicek, 2017), more recent scholarship is interested in platformisation as a mechanism for capitalisation and speculation, where the ownership of assets overrides other forms of value creation. This emphasis on assets enables platformisation to be projected towards an ever-receding future of promised revenues enabled by the efficiencies, automations, and superior knowledge of data and AI. This future orientation entails a distinctive "mode of techno-economic ordering" manifested in concrete business strategies and accounting innovations – a form of "techcraft" (Birch et al., 2021) that represents an alternative to traditional notions of accumulation and commodification (Birch & Muniesa, 2020; Sadowski, 2019).

The promissory narratives of platformisation manifest in education in two ways: through the already mentioned "futuring" of edtech investors which creates concrete opportunities for future cash flows in education, but more importantly through the appropriation of the intrinsic future orientation of education. After all, the possibility of multiple and divergent futures is embedded in the very fabric of this institution. Education is a promise of a better future. Piggybacking on first-order educational futures, platformisation articulates its own second-order promises: personalised learning for all, bridging achievement gaps, more motivated and engaged students, and so forth. This double promising that so effectively capitalises on the "future bias" of education is what makes platformisation so appealing in this sector and explains its symbolic and economic value. Its influence can be observed in multiple technological solutions pledging to address chronic educational problems rendered "wicked" by decades of institutional ossification: rigid curricula out of touch with the world of industry, low student engagement, heavy teacher workloads, and so forth. It is crucial however that the imaginary and future-facing nature of platformed education is not viewed as more important than the actual reality of "infrastructuring", understood as the fluid and iterative materialisation of its future visions.

Infrastructuring

In 1854, the Metropolitan Railway (the Met) was granted permission by the English government to build a subterranean line at an estimated cost of £1 million. On the first day, during the inauguration, there were six derailments caused by misalignments of the tracks (Wolmar, 2012). This incident was one of the key historical factors that led, in 1863, to the development of the 4-foot-8-inch gauge as the de facto standard in the railway industry, which enabled trains and railway tracks to inter-operate, thus reducing derailments and saving considerable costs. Before the widespread adoption of the track gauge standard, it was common for trains departing from a location to be unloaded in another station because the tracks and the train wheels would not align. With the introduction of a common gauge standard, trains could be smoothly "plugged" into the infrastructure and leave and depart without disruption. This key historical episode illustrates that the development of infrastructures relies heavily on technological conformity: the integration and coordination of systems so that they may operate cohesively, enhancing efficiency and overall effectiveness. Infrastructural conformity is attained in two interrelated ways. First, by designing compatible technological components, such as interlocking railway tracks or, to use a more recent example, matching internet ports and cables that enable wired networking (e.g., Gigabit Ethernet). Second, infrastructuring requires the development of "abstract entities such as protocols (human and computer), standards, and memory" (Bowker et al., 2010, p. 93). As Bowker and colleagues noted in their now classic work, synchronised and standardised infrastructures usually operate behind the scenes, which means that the human labour to build and maintain them does not always receive sufficient recognition or visibility. Because of their nature as a substrate, it can be hard to see the impact and political implications of infrastructures, but their influence on multiple forms of social life is undeniable. This influence engenders homogenisation on a grand scale and is animated by a desire for control, efficiency, and predictability.

As briefly mentioned in the introductory chapter, the defining characteristic of all infrastructures is their tendency to operate as a standardised framework for social life. However, this does not occur in rigid and overly constraining ways, but by providing parameters within which sociotechnical relations can occur with a degree of flexibility. The notion of active form (Easterling, 2014) can help us make sense of this key feature. According to

Easterling, the socially constitutive function of infrastructure is not enacted through a linear design logic, but by establishing active forms that generate "dispositions", understood as

> the character or propensity of an organization that results from all its activity. It is the medium, not the message. It is not the pattern printed on the fabric but the way the fabric floats. It is not the shape of the game piece but the way the game piece plays. It is not the text but the constantly updating software that manages the text. Not the object form, but the active form.
>
> *(p. 14)*

An example of active form is the multiplier, where a single infrastructural element – for example, the car in the suburban context – precipitates the development of other elements: local roads, highways, garages, driveways, front-gardens and so on. Following the French philosopher Jean Baudrillard, the car should be viewed in this instance less as an artefact (its object form) than as a "system of signs" (Baudrillard, 2005). Baudrillard examined two dimensions of artefacts, which can be described through linguistic concepts. The structural dimension denotes the physical characteristics of an artefact, akin to the primary or direct meaning of words in linguistics. Baudrillard suggested that this denotative aspect can only be analysed abstractly, because an object's material integrity is constantly influenced by cultural dynamics, which he equated with the linguistic process of connotation. Thus, objects are in "perpetual flight from their technical structure (denotation) towards their secondary meanings, from the technological system towards a cultural system (connotation)" (p. 6). It is at this level of cultural connotation that the object form turns into an active form, acting as a generator of activities and dispositions that enable large-scale infrastructures to come into being.

Active forms like the multiplier operate as the software of infrastructure: not what objects are in a material sense, but what objects do or enable to do. Unlike static entities, software acts autonomously or in response to user inputs, performing sequences of operations that transform or generate information. Unsurprisingly, this generative logic has been fully rendered in the digital domain through so-called middleware: actual software that acts as an intermediary and a multiplier, facilitating coordination between components which may be running on different machines or platforms. Middleware "multiplies" infrastructure by enabling a great deal of repetitive activities across platform ecosystems: data retrieval, data modification, user authentication, payment transactions, social interactions, machine learning integration and related analytics, and more. The standardised multiplication enabled by middleware helps us to understand the role of the platform as an agnostic technology that operates at scale – a node positioned at the intersection of data flows, multiplying/facilitating interactions, and transactions between human and non-human parties. A particular form of middleware – application programming interfaces (APIs) – is central in this multiplicative dynamic and deserves to be examined more in detail.

APIs are essentially structured sets of programming rules and data parameters that enable external applications to seamlessly integrate with a platform (Helmond, 2015). Major companies like Facebook and Amazon have popularised API usage and have significantly benefitted from the associated business models. APIs have been pivotal in establishing an "industry-wide practice of controlled openness and interoperability among social media services" (Bodle, 2011, p. 329). They are crucial infrastructure elements in the process of platformisation. Thanks to the mediation of APIs, third-party entities (small developers, large vendors, service providers) are enrolled as a source of innovation and labour. Additionally, they transform end-user interactions into opportunities for data collection. When developing an API, its creators must "foresee" various scenarios in which people, devices, and different data types engage in (largely) predetermined ways. Such "ontological work" is performed by abstracting complex social relationships in the interest of commensurability and algorithmic efficiency.

For example, the Mechanical Turk API, Amazon's proprietary API that connects workers, employers ("requesters") and data structures to enable standardised "clickworking" tasks – known as Human Intelligence Tasks (HITs) – constantly and dynamically engineers an abstract market where human labour can be bought and sold without frictions. HITs can range from data validation and content moderation to image tagging and sentiment analysis. The process begins by crafting a HIT, defining its title, description, and reward structure. Through the API, it is then possible to meticulously define the prerequisites workers must meet to participate, and monitor the HIT in real time, checking how many are completed, how many are in progress, and how many are pending review. In short, the API gives full control and visibility over the labour process. Facebook's Social Graph API operates in a comparable manner, transforming individuals and their diverse social interactions into continuously accessible and traceable "entities" (likes, updates, histories, etc.), all of which are imbued with economic value (Bucher, 2012). For developers seeking to integrate Facebook's social elements into their applications, the process begins with obtaining an access token – a digital credential for accessing Facebook's data. Armed with this token, developers can traverse the Social Graph, retrieving user profiles, friend lists, and other data. This functionality can be used to power various applications, such as those that recommend content based on a user's social connections.

Digital infrastructuring in education: The role of APIs

As illustrated in the previous section, APIs are infrastructural linchpins that carry out a crucial function of mediation, translation, and harmonisation. Their design is often accompanied by a promotional rhetoric of ease of use and efficiency. In education, this rhetoric was played out with strategic effectiveness when two of the foremost technology giants (Google and Amazon) colonised schools and universities through an infrastructural strategy where APIs were central. At the turn of the millennium, Google strategically decided to venture into the edtech sector, thus broadening its ever-expanding array of digital initiatives. Initially known as "Apps for Education", this venture was later renamed GSuite for Education. This expansion was further enhanced by the release of Google's cost-effective Chromebooks in 2011 and the debut of Google Classroom in 2014. In 2015, Google's educational initiative advanced into its next phase with the launch of the Classroom API. Jonathan Rochelle, the company's ex-product director for education, unveiled the API at the International Society for Technology in Education (ISTE) conference in Philadelphia. He described the API as a platform enabling connections among developers, educators, and students. The primary objective of the API was to integrate Google's services and infrastructure into the educational sector, promoting the development of a cloud-based technological ecosystem with various third-party applications. Rochelle, discussing the API's launch, commented:

> it fits so well into our strength and ease of deployment. It's definitely much simpler than having the servers in the school, that's like a no-brainer these days. This hits administrators and the school district and school boards as something really powerful.
>
> *(Shueh, 2015 paragraph 9)*

This trajectory towards a fully integrated API ecosystem culminated in 2021 with another rebranding: G Suite for education became Google Workspace for Education. The rebranding reinforced the narrative of seamless and care-free integration, with teachers promised instantaneous access to "favourite EdTech tools and content from a marketplace" (Lazare, 2021 n.p.), and a stronger emphasis on analytics and data tracking "to give teachers visibility into which students are engaged and which are falling behind" (ibid.).

Like Google, Amazon has a strong interest in the education business, framing its cloud-based technologies as capable of granting educational institutions access to advanced analytical functionalities without specialist expertise. "They're just plug-and-play. You don't have to get into all the weeds and get the training data and label the data and all those sort of things", the vice-president for AI of Amazon Web Services (AWS – the Amazon subsidiary that offers cloud-based functionalities on a pay-as-you-go basis) was reported saying (Shah, 2019). Using such tools, any organisation can mobilise AI-based predictive technology to extract valuable insights from datasets, without having to engage with the costly complexities of data science. The official promotional language of AWS is worth quoting:

> The AWS Cloud frees schools and districts from the distractions of managing infrastructure, reduces risk, and improves digital equity so they can focus on students. With the AWS Cloud, schools and districts can access industry-shaping technology at an affordable cost, no matter the scale. From back-end data management to virtual desktops, AWS offers tools so that every student gets the attention they need to thrive.
>
> *(AWS, 2021, p. 10)*

There is a recurring emphasis on convenience, efficiency, ease of deployment and "no-brainer decisions" in these statements, which is, of course, directly related to the plug-and-play imaginary and its promissory narratives. What is missing are the implications of public sector institutions being recast as interchangeable tenants, who hire software architectures on a pay-as-you-go basis and plug their operations into multiple sockets while remaining oblivious of the interests, negotiations, and technical complexities that lie just beyond. The entire process is, of course, mediated by APIs (the sockets) that allow institutional platforms to interface with proprietary infrastructures. In the case of AWS, a complex "API Gateway" governs multiple data flows, allowing "thousands of system integrators and tens of thousands of independent software vendors (…) to sync their products" (AWS, 2023).

It is important to note at this point that this discourse of ease of use and fuzzy obliviousness is not exclusive to contemporary data infrastructures. Geoffrey Bowker and Leigh Star wrote about it in a seminal book that sought to reveal the invisible sociotechnical arrangements that undergird all forms of infrastructure development and utilisation. They used the phrase "as if by magic" to capture the sense of mundane wonder that colours our daily engagement with infrastructures (Bowker et al., 2010, p. 97). As "regular" users, we are not required to understand how these infrastructures work, and most importantly we have a very limited notion of the tensions and contestations that hide behind their semblance of functional smoothness. In their now-classic investigation, Bowker and Star set out to dispel some of that magic by examining several – deceptively prosaic – descriptive questions: How do things fit and operate together to create the guise of efficiency and ease of use? Who performs the upkeep labour that underpins ease of use?

24 Platformed education

What happens when something or someone does not "fit" and a few cracks begin to appear on the otherwise smooth surfaces of these systems?

Following Bowker and Star, we can therefore appreciate the key political role of invisibility in all infrastructures, which has been bolstered by digitisation and is now leading to what the French anthropologist Levi Strauss called "fabulation" (Lévi-Strauss, 2016): a phenomenon where something that has been deliberately rendered invisible (a sleight of hand) can become a political tool that governs by generating compelling narratives of superhuman intervention. Lévi-Strauss believed that the process of fabulation involves taking disparate elements and weaving them into a coherent narrative that helps us understand our surroundings. These narratives often incorporate magic, mythology, and fantastical intervention, serving as a way for societies to explain natural and social phenomena that might otherwise seem inexplicable. While the shamans of old would draw on myths and religion to imbue their "magical" practices with power, platformisation – through the intricacies of datafication and infrastructuring – achieves the same result by hiding the bias and fallibility of its operations behind a façade of objectivity, buttressed by a rhetoric of more-than-human analytical capabilities. Through this "algorithmic fabulation", platformisation reengineers institutions in the interest of efficiency and prediction. Schools and universities willingly join in, operationalising all aspects of their core functions as data and then allowing external parties to access those data through various plug-and-play openings where organisational processes, values and practices disappear as inputs, to then return "as if by magic" in the form of insights, recommendations and predictions.

Platformed participation

All infrastructures are ultimately meant to host social life: they are contexts where people – or "end users" as they are sometimes called – participate. Infrastructural elements create specific templates for participation shaping the interactions occurring within and across the platformisation landscape. A "classic" conceptualisation of participation was proposed during the early years of the platformisation boom (Fish et al., 2011). It distinguished between the top-down control enacted by a Formal Social Enterprise (FSE), understood as a structured governing entity (a corporation or government agency), and the bottom-up agency of Organised Publics (OPs), understood as social groups that come together according to fluid criteria of cultural affinity or economic interest. The tensions and the negotiations between FSEs and OPs determine the extent to which a platform is participatory. In a situation of highly structured participation, FSEs exercise tight control over user interactions and content. This form of participation is characterised by prescriptive rules, strict content moderation, and centralised decision-making, with clear guidelines, enforced content policies, and algorithms that curate and filter user-generated content. This approach aims to maintain a high degree of order, ensuring compliance with legal and community standards. In a situation of managed participation, governance structures are more flexible, allowing organised publics a degree of autonomy within well-defined boundaries. Users have the freedom to generate content and interact with others, but their actions are subject to oversight to ensure that community standards are upheld.

Initial conceptualisations of participation were relatively optimistic in their belief that it was possible to have free and bottom-up agency within and across platforms. The progressive establishment of business models based on algorithmic surveillance and data monetisation during the 2010s undermined this belief considerably, giving rise to a more critical outlook where the very notion of free platformed participation became a quasi-oxymoron. This critical outlook is exemplified by the notion of "milieu-based governance" (Andrejevic, 2020), which largely refers to platform logics where "action is brought to bear on the rules of the game rather than on the players" (Foucault et al., 2008, pp. 259–260). This type of governance shapes participation by subtly "modulating" the conditions in which people operate. Widespread strategies include behavioural nudging, sentiment manipulation, algorithmic curation, incentives structures, and reputation systems. As we live within and across platformed contexts, milieu-based governance steers participation in the interest of efficiency and value extraction, influencing how people reason, act, and communicate within a predefined decision space. As a result, we participate either by internalising goals and actively contributing (through free labour) to the platform's business model as it aligns with personal interests, or by forgoing agency altogether as we offload an increasing number of responsibilities onto automated systems, which then regulate and govern unbeknownst to all but the most technically minded and privacy-conscious among us.

> If disciplinary control thrived on the homogeneity of mass society, environmental governance relies on the range and diversity of the post-mass moment: the goal is not to enforce behavioral norms but to unleash the full range of activity that will allow patterns to emerge as clearly as possible in order to correlate, predict, and pre-empt.
>
> *(Andrejevic, 2020, p. 40)*

"Engagement" is one of the key metrics upon which the viability of milieu-based governance depends. This functional dependence on user engagement and the associated psycho-social mechanism – attention – amounts to a passive form of value creation, where economic worth is created not through innovation, but by entrapping people's time and commitment. Indeed, even when a platform offers a useful service, the continued improvement of that service is secondary to the social engagement that emerges around it. An example from the multibillion videogames industry illustrates this point. Nowadays, millions of people regularly take part in sophisticated social interactions in the context of free-to-play multiplayer video games, which, unlike traditional single-player experiences, operate more like platformed entertainment services. Interactions in these "games" range from purchasing and trading virtual cosmetic items, to collaborative strategies to beat the game, to various forms of synchronous and asynchronous communication: live chatrooms, forums, fan-made wikis, gameplay streaming, and so forth. Such interactions are shaped by trends, "memes", and real-life events, like the virtual live performances from world-famous artists that take place in the popular video game Fortnite. These events do not bring improvements to the gameplay – the "core" dimension of any video game, which in Fortnite's case has remained largely unchanged since 2017 – but are designed to enhance the environmental and cultural conditions that drive up community engagement, which in turn leads to more "microtransactions" and thus concrete financial gains. To be sure, there are now opportunities in Fortnite to simply hang out without taking part in competitive gameplay at all, while still partaking in the collective sociality simulated within the shared world and facilitated by its attendant economy. The Fortnite infrastructure is therefore designed to provide psychological and affective rewards for engaging with the game, where engagement is an ever-expanding transmedia and cross-platform category that incorporates informal sociality, spectating, creating and sharing content, and so forth.

This model – let's call it engagement engineering – is the real innovation that emerged from the fandom-driven gaming industry well before social media behemoths like Facebook adopted them as a key component of their business strategy: the more people are personally invested in a digital ecosystem, the more value is generated. This functional addiction to engagement has, however, a dark side. A valuable service, like a compelling gameplay loop or a useful interface to stay in touch with friends and relatives, plays an important role in attracting users. As such, an initial investment in its quality is crucial even if it means operating at a loss for a period. This continues until users develop significant personal or economic stakes in the platform so that leaving it becomes inconvenient or downright damaging. Once participation has reached a certain magnitude and it is viewed by platform owners as sufficiently "locked in", monetisation begins: complex fee structures, invasively personalised advertising, "boosting" schemes that provide access to paywalled functionalities, and so forth. This is the "path of enshittification" theorised by the technology critic and writer Cory Doctorow, which eventually leads to user exodus and to the "crepuscular senescence of dying platforms" (Doctorow, 2023, p. n.p.). This brief synthesis of the critical scholarship and commentary about platformed participation raises an obvious question: how, if at all, does it apply to education?

Platformed participation in education

In his book *Failure to Disrupt: Why Technology Alone Can't Transform Education* (Reich, 2020), Justin Reich identifies three genres of edtech based on the question: who creates the activity sequence for learners? If an instructor is in charge, then we have Learning Management Systems and certain types of Massively Open Online Courses (MOOCs); if the activity sequence is assembled by an algorithm, then we have Intelligent or adaptive tutoring systems; if the sequence is assembled by a peer, we have distributed learning networks of interest, such as communities of content creators. This is a simple, yet elegant, taxonomy that can help us conceptualise the nature of platformed educational participation. In the first genre, participation is modelled after the well-established templates of formal educational structures. On the educator side: delivering lessons in a presentational format, designing assessment tasks, grading student work; on the student side: attending classes, engaging with readings, completing and submitting coursework. This very specific form of engagement has very little in common with the way participation has been theorised in platform studies. The only element that remains is the emphasis on scale and access: the same type of "instructionist" educational participation that we know well, but able to reach thousands if not millions, and significantly cheaper on account of digitally enabled efficiencies and automations (e.g., video recorded content, automated grading and immediate feedback on tasks). It was what xMOOCs (eXtended Massive Open Online Courses) promised, and unsurprisingly they have been entirely assimilated by the existing higher education system. As such, they

> have neither conquered the world nor gone bust. Instead, they plod along, adopting forms and business models – like OPMs or executive education[1] – that are recognizable to those familiar with the history of online learning in higher education over the last two decades.
>
> *(Reich, 2020, p. 33)*

In the second genre (algorithm-based instruction), Reich places adaptive tutors like Khan Academy, where pre-developed educational content and extra remedial support is presented to individual users according to real-time adaptation to human performance. In this genre, there is hardly any participation at all, not even the abstracted and asynchronous recreation of classroom interaction and dialogue found in xMOOCs. This is a type of educational technology steeped in an individualistic and cybernetic vision of one-to-one tuition that hearkens back to the "teaching machines" devised by B.F. Skinner in the 1950s (Watters, 2021).

In the third genre – peer-based learning – we finally have something that resembles the participation of organised publics. Reich's idea of peer-based learning is moulded after theories of the networked society (Castells, 2009) and by the somewhat related notions of participatory and situated learning that played a significant role in the early enthusiasm for the educational potential of the internet (Lave & Wenger, 1991; Sfard, 1998). Echoes of this approach can be found in initiatives like the MIT-sponsored Scratch, which enables millions of young users around the world to learn the basics of software programming by creating and sharing content. However, it's the failure of the connectivist MOOCs (cMOOCs) that catches Reich's attention and indeed ours. cMOOCs – not to be confused with xMOOCs, which belong to the instructionist genre described earlier – are informed by a principled pursuit of decentralisation and openness, and encourage a form of social learning that relies on the self-organising power of networked communities (Downes, 2008). They quickly emerged at the end of the 2000s, "in the pivot point between a dramatic increase in the number of people creating content online and the capture of all that activity by a handful of proprietary platforms" (Reich, 2020, p. 86). In this sense, their demise at the hands of the combined forces of ambitious corporate xMOOCs and meddling university administrators can be viewed as one of the earliest instances of the sort of platform decay described by Doctorow.

Reich's edtech taxonomy helps us appreciate how the trajectory of platformed educational participation is familiar and distinctive at the same time. On the one hand, the concept can be subsumed under long-running disagreements about pedagogy and learning: individualism vs. collectivism, and expert guidance vs. autonomous discovery. As a result, traditional forms of educational participation (e.g., one-to-many instruction) are still alive and well in many edtech platforms. On the other hand, platformed educational participation reflects the assimilation of an imaginary of distributed agency which, as noted earlier, is associated with the network society and its "connectivist" affordances. This duality causes a Janus-like dynamic: one side of educational platformisation faces the status quo, partially or fully congruent with the pre-existing arrangements of teaching, learning, and administration; the second face of platformed educational participation looks beyond formal institutions and their change-resistant structures, and is indeed oriented to the future, animated by a vision of granular, on-demand alignment between individual interests and economic opportunity. In the first scenario, the underlying foundations remain unchanged, as the platformed infrastructures of edtech do not introduce new forms of educational participation. Instead, they seek to streamline and automate that which was already there. Thus, the "gameplay" (teaching, learning, and the complex administrative dynamics of education) is the same, but the datafied "premium" experience built around such gameplay justifies the profitable tenancy agreements that provide states, districts, and institutions with access to advanced back-end analytics and automations. The second scenario is no less consequential. Even though it was never fully realised and often failed under the weight of its own aspirations, with cMOOCs in particular representing the "road not taken" according to Reich (2020, p. 87), connectivism is still a powerful discursive rationale that drives the marketing and expansion of educational platformisation. Its primary objective is to bring into reality an educational vision of networked individualism, where people participate by becoming entangled with platform ecosystems that promise future benefits and rewards, but demand in return a great deal of personal motivation, investment, and self-regulation. It is precisely in this stipulation that the distinctive educational proposition of platformisation is located. It is so central to the argument developed in this book that it deserves its own dedicated discussion in the next chapter.

Conclusion

As this chapter comes to its conclusion, I wish to reflect further on how the concepts that I described here have – directly or indirectly – shaped the scholarly debate around platformisation in education. After decades of unwarranted enthusiasm and unproven claims about the power of technology to enhance sociality and learning, it became clear that the large-scale datafication of society ushered in by the internet resulted in problems and tensions. Many began to realise that unlimited access to knowledge goes hand in hand with reduced trust in epistemic authority, that "memetic" shallowness may undermine the ability to engage deeply with knowledge, and that intensely emotional (and poorly moderated) online participation exacerbates political divisions and the ensuing incommunicability between ideologically diverse groups. The list of misgivings goes on. Against this background, critical social researchers with an interest in education – myself included – have produced various accounts which, I believe, can be broadly divided into two alternative interpretations. In the first one, contemporary global education is onto a path towards oppressive large-scale surveillance and privatisation. Converging around this view are several strands of critical social enquiry that consider public education in many countries as irremediably compromised by decades of neoliberal interference and underfunding, which paved

30 Platformed education

the way for digitisation and then platformisation as not-so-subtle attempts to crack open the sector and allow the insertion of market forces.

The second reading is equally critical in tone but is also more open to compromise by advancing a notion of platformed education as a disordered "assemblage", rather than a coherent political-economic project. According to this second view, platformed education is not a unitary political-economic project but a sociotechnical "mess" susceptible to fragmentation and diversification. Within this framework, various agents employ technologies for surveillance, evaluation, and regulation, frequently operating in isolation: inspection agencies, national and international assessment frameworks, classification and ranking systems, computational methods for "learning analytics", and, notably, an expanding sector of edtech apps and digital platforms. Differences between the global north and south further exacerbate this heterogeneity, and indeed the political economy of platformed education reflects broader geopolitical factors, even though the underlying infrastructure is global in reach and largely mono-cultural, that is, US-centric and English-speaking. Other regions, for instance, the Asia-Pacific, are treated as "growth markets" with local education systems rapidly establishing links with technology providers and creating multiple dependencies in the process. Sectoral differences also abound with large interoperable infrastructures rapidly emerging in "entrepreneurial" higher education institutions in English-speaking countries. Meanwhile, in most national K-12 sectors platformisation must cohabit with volatile collections of local policies reflecting the long-running and often pre-digital politics of curriculum and pedagogy: conservatism vs. progressivism, vocational vs. academic, selectivity vs. inclusion and multiple contestations around the reproduction of inequality through education.

In sum, there are two equally legitimate positions that a critical observer could take in relation to platformisation in education: a compellingly linear explanation that configures a clear, if rather blunt, form of political agency based on critique and resistance; and more indeterminate position that contemplates the creative potential of heterogeneity. The advantage of the latter line of thought, compared to the former, is that an "imperfect panopticon" cannot always and under all circumstances be the result of clear-cut malicious intentions, because it is too "underdetermined" by multiple sociotechnical influences. As such, educational technology infrastructures – viewed as fractured and iterative accumulation of relational enactments – could in principle be "reverse engineered" by foregrounding the work involved in their making. This "infrastructural inversion" (Bowker & Star, 1999) can, on the one hand, inform a critical public debate about the ideological and political pitfalls of platformisation; on the other hand, it may help us redefine notions of design and usage in a more inclusive and socially just way.

At the same time, we should not dismiss the opportunities of platformisation out of hand, as the data-based personalisation enabled by digital platforms has a role to play in contemporary education. The crucial question is therefore whether surveillance capitalism is the only possible template for this role. This may well be the case, but it cannot be accepted as an inevitability.

Note

1 Online Program Managers (OPMs) are companies that develop conventional online courses and degrees in partnership with universities, following an outsourcing model where the OPM takes on most design and delivery functions under the brand of the partner institution. Executive education refers to short, non- credentialed professional courses that focus for the most part on business skills.

References

Andrejevic, M. (2020). *Automated media*. Routledge.
AWS. (2021). *Innovation for life: State and local governments and education powered by the cloud*. Amazon Web Services Retrieved October 4, 2023 from https://pages.awscloud.com/rs/112-TZM-766/images/AWS_Innovaton_for_Life_eBook.pdf?did=psr_card&trk=psr_card
AWS. (2023). *What is AWS*. Retrieved October 4, 2023 from https://aws.amazon.com/what-is-aws/
Baudrillard, J. (2005). *The system of objects*. Verso.
Beer, D. (2018). *The data gaze: Capitalism, power and perception*. Sage.
Birch, K., Cochrane, D., & Ward, C. (2021). Data as asset? The measurement, governance, and valuation of digital personal data by Big Tech. *Big Data & Society*, *8*(1). https://doi.org/10.1177/20539517211017308
Birch, K., & Muniesa, F. (2020). *Assetization: Turning things into assets in technoscientific capitalism*. MIT Press.
Bodle, R. (2011). Regimes of sharing. *Information, Communication & Society*, *14*(3), 320–337. https://doi.org/10.1080/1369118X.2010.542825
Bowker, G. C., Baker, K., Millerand, F., & Ribes, D. (2010). Toward information infrastructure studies: Ways of knowing in a networked environment. In J. Hunsinger, L. Klastrup, & M. Allen (Eds.), *International handbook of internet research* (pp. 97–117). Springer. https://doi.org/10.1007/978-1-4020-9789-8
Bowker, G. C., & Star, S. L. (1999). *Sorting things out: Classification and its consequences*. MIT Press.
Bratton, B. H. (2015). *The stack: On software and sovereignty*. MIT Press. https://doi.org/10.7551/mitpress/9780262029575.001.0001
Bucher, T. (2012). Want to be on the top? Algorithmic power and the threat of invisibility on Facebook. *New Media & Society*, *14*(7), 1164–1180. https://doi.org/10.1177/1461444812440159
Castells, M. (2009). *The rise of the network society*. Wiley. https://doi.org/10.1002/9781444319514

32 Platformed education

Darrough, M., & Ye, J. (2007). Valuation of loss firms in a knowledge-based economy. *Review of Accounting Studies*, *12*, 61–93. https://doi.org/10.2139/ssrn.902694

Deleuze, G., & Guattari, F. (1988). *A thousand plateaus: Capitalism and Schizophrenia.* Bloomsbury Publishing.

Doctorow, C. (2023). The 'Enshittification' of TikTok Or how, exactly, platforms die. *WIRED* Retrieved November 15, 2023, from https://www.wired.com/story/tiktok-platforms-cory-doctorow/

Downes, S. (2008). Places to go: Connectivism & Connective Knowledge. *Innovate: Journal of Online Education*, *5*(1), 6. Retrieved November 15, 2023, from https://nsuworks.nova.edu/innovate/vol5/iss1/6/

Easterling, K. (2014). *Extrastatecraft: The power of infrastructure space.* Verso Books.

Fish, A., Murillo, L. F. R., Nguyen, L., Panofsky, A., & Kelty, C. M. (2011). Birds of the Internet. *Journal of Cultural Economy*, *4*(2), 157–187. https://doi.org/10.1080/17530350.2011.563069

Foucault, M., Burchell, G., & Davidson, A. (2008). *The birth of biopolitics: Lectures at the Collège de France, 1978–1979.* New York, NY: Springer.

Gulson, K. N., & Sellar, S. (2019). Emerging data infrastructures and the new topologies of education policy. *Environment and Planning D: Society and Space*, *37*(2), 350–366. https://doi.org/10.1177/0263775818813144

Gulson, K. N., & Webb, P. T. (2017). Mapping an emergent field of 'computational education policy': Policy rationalities, prediction and data in the age of Artificial Intelligence. *Research in Education*, *98*(1), 14–26. https://doi.org/10.1177/0034523717723385

Hartong, S., & Piattoeva, N. (2021). Contextualizing the datafication of schooling–a comparative discussion of Germany and Russia. *Critical Studies in Education*, *62*(2), 227–242. https://doi.org/10.1080/17508487.2019.1618887

Helmond, A. (2015). The Platformization of the Web: Making Web Data Platform Ready. *Social Media + Society*, *1*(2), 1–11. https://doi.org/10.1177/2056305115603080

Holloway, J., & Lewis, S. (2022). Governing teachers through datafication: Physical–virtual hybridity and language interoperability in teacher accountability. *Big Data & Society*, *9*(2). https://doi.org/10.1177/20539517221137553

Jasanoff, S., & Kim, S.-H. (2015). *Dreamscapes of modernity: Sociotechnical imaginaries and the fabrication of power.* University of Chicago Press.

Jones, B. O. (1990). *Sleepers, wake! Technology and the future of work.* Oxford University Press.

Lave, J., & Wenger, E. (1991). *Situated learning: Legitimate peripheral participation.* Cambridge University Press.

Lazare, M. (2021). *A peek at what's next for Google Classroom.* Google Retrieved 5/09/2023 from https://blog.google/outreach-initiatives/education/classroom-road map/

Lem, S. (2014). *The cyberiad: Fables for the cybernetic age.* Penguin, UK.

Levina, M., & Hasinoff, A. A. (2017). The silicon valley ethos: Tech industry products, discourses, and practices. *Television & New Media*, *18*(6), 489–495. https://doi.org/10.1177/1527476416680454

Lévi-Strauss, C. (2016). The Sorcerer and his magic. In P. Brown & S. Closser (Eds.), *Understanding and applying medical anthropology* (pp. 197–203). Routledge.

Morozov, E. (2013). *To save everything, click here: The folly of technological solutionism* (1st ed.). PublicAffairs.

Noble, D. (1999). *The religion of technology: The divinity of man and the spirit of invention*. Penguin Books.

Reich, J. (2020). *Failure to disrupt: Why technology alone can't transform education*. Harvard University Press.

Sadowski, J. (2019). When data is capital: Datafication, accumulation, and extraction. *Big Data and Society*, 6(1). https://doi.org/10.1177/2053951718820549

Sfard, A. (1998). On two metaphors for learning and the dangers of choosing just one. *Educational Researcher*, 27(2), 4–13. https://doi.org/10.2307/1176193

Shah, A. (2019, June 19). *Amazon Introduces 'Plug and Play' AI Tools*. Dow Jones Publications. Retrieved October 4, 2023 from https://www.wsj.com/articles/amazon-introduces-plug-and-play-ai-tools-11575399371

Shueh, J. (2015). *Google Classroom Update Opens Platform to Education Developers, Publishers*. Government Technology. Retrieved June 1, 2023 from https://www.govtech.com/education/Google-Classroom-Update-Opens-Platform-to-Education-Developers-Publishers.html

Sims, C. (2017). *Disruptive fixation*. Princeton University Press.

Srnicek, N. (2017). *Platform capitalism*. Pollity.

Watters, A. (2021). *Teaching machines: The history of personalized learning*. MIT Press.

Williamson, B. (2017). *Big data in education: The digital future of learning, policy and practice*. Sage.

Williamson, B., & Komljenovic, J. (2023). Investing in imagined digital futures: The techno-financial 'futuring' of edtech investors in higher education. *Critical Studies in Education*, 64(3), 234–249. https://doi.org/10.1080/17508487.2022.2081587

Wolmar, C. (2012). *The subterranean railway how the London Underground was built and how it changed the city forever*. Atlantic Books.

3

EDUCATING IN PLATFORMS

Is platformisation a transformative moment in the history of educational theory and practice?

While several desirable outcomes are often associated with platformisation – personalisation, efficiency, flexibility, access and so forth – the actual nature of platformed education remains vague. To a significant extent, this is caused by the emphasis on agnostic mediation of platformisation, which eschews theoretical allegiances and pursues a sort of epistemological plasticity where multiple pedagogical paradigms can be folded within each other: the "promise" of platformisation is that it can adapt to multiple different forms of education. What this promise actually does, however, is shine a light on a chronic difficulty in education writ large, a field where theoretical and practical approaches have coexisted and vied for prominence for centuries, with countless fads and a few enduring philosophical orientations that often reflect deep cultural differences.

Despite such variability, there is a "dominant" model of education, which presupposes a developmental progression from lower to higher cognitive stages, facilitated by more experienced others and occurring in regimented times and spaces designed to enable the rational management of large populations of students. Encircling this mainstream model there is a literal constellation of frameworks that extends in all possible directions: education as political emancipation, education as individual self-help and growth, education as sociocultural participation in communities of practice, education as "becoming" and identity formation, and much more. Some of these paradigms are aligned with the mainstream model; others challenge it in explicit

DOI: 10.4324/9781003099826-3

or implicit ways, for instance by advocating the priority of informal membership over formal and structured learning. It is impossible to do justice to the diversity and often contradictory nature of educational theory in a single volume, let alone a chapter. Some choices, informed by research questions, are needed.

The question that interests me here is whether platformisation represents a transformative moment in the history of educational theory and practice – an innovation that introduced genuinely novel approaches to foster learning and knowledge advancement. To answer this query, I will draw on three disciplinary perspectives to develop a theoretical account of platformed education:

1. Learning Sciences – In the first instance, I will examine one of the most widespread and influential paradigms in educational psychology, considering its historical trajectory and its thematic and "operational" affinity with platformisation: self-regulated learning.
2. Curriculum Studies – second, I will examine the issue of worthwhile knowledge in relation to platformisation, to then consider the hidden ramifications in terms of socialisation, subjectification, and habituation. To this purpose, I will describe the concept of "infrastructural curriculum".
3. Social Anthropology – third, I will draw on scholarship that conceptualises learning as a process of coordination and tension occurring within spatial-temporal configurations. In this perspective, platformisation acts as a topological configuration requiring its "inhabitants" to develop pragmatic and political strategies of living and dwelling.

Learning science: Is platformed learning a form of self-regulated learning?

Self-regulation is a fundamental evolutionary quality of all living organisms. It refers to the capacity to develop biological and behavioural patterns which can successfully adapt to the environment. The self-regulation principle applies to the entire lifespan, with early years self-regulation mostly concerned with foundational skills such as attentional control and emotion regulation (Bronson & Bronson, 2001), and adult self-regulation implicated in self-directed agency, goal setting, and metacognition (Pintrich & Zusho, 2007). In less developed species and infants, self-regulation is for the most part a reactive process initiated when external and internal stimuli create the appropriate conditions for regulating a response. It is important to make a distinction between the response itself and the organisation, modification, and correction of that response, which occurs as the organism interacts with the environment.

Self-regulation is primarily about the latter, but the resulting feedback loop changes – or has the potential to change – the nature of the original response. As internal biological systems and social conditions increase in complexity during the life course, self-regulation becomes more proactive and, in the case of humans, the result of deliberate planning and "metacognitive" control (Boekaerts & Niemivirta, 2000). The ability to modulate one's cognitive resources, redirecting intellectual and emotional energy towards shifting priorities, lies at the heart of modern developmental psychology, including Piagetian and post-Piagetian approaches which had a great deal of influence on contemporary educational practice (Piaget, 2002; Von Glasersfeld, 2013).

Likewise, the notion of adaptive self-regulation facilitated through social and cultural "scaffolding" plays an important role in the Vygotskian and post-Vygotskian traditions (Bruner, 1986; Vygotsky & Cole, 1978). Self-regulation underpins several other successful psychological frameworks, such as those that stress the significance of intrinsic motivation to enable personal growth and self-determination (Deci & Ryan, 2008; Haimovitz & Dweck, 2017). Self-regulation, in short, is ubiquitous in educational theory and practice, certainly thanks to the validating effect of a large body of empirical evidence, but also on account of its applied implications: self-regulation can be taught and learnt. Thus, the umbrella notion of self-regulated learning (SRL) emerged as a framework for educational interventions involving several individual-level factors that influence adaptive effectiveness in education: self-efficacy, malleable (non-fixed) intelligence, internal motivation, and metacognitive dispositions towards a sense of mastery.

The popularity of self-regulation in education has also something to do with social values, as this notion is predicated on the priority of human agency and autonomy, standing in contrast with other explanatory frameworks that place greater weight on external forces or internal, uncontrollable drives. These include sociological accounts that emphasise the role of economic and cultural structures, but, as far as educational theory is concerned, SRL developed mostly as a reaction to behaviourism, which informed a much more forceful and controlling approach to human development, overly reliant on biological or external rewards and, as such, fostering passivity rather than agentic control over learning and life in general. The rise of cybernetics after the Second World War (Wiener, 1961/2019) also played a part in this rejection, as behaviourists' antipathy towards explanatory models of internal functioning collided with evidence about the role of feedback loops, understood as intrinsic mechanisms which enable self-regulating systems (organisms and machines) to interact autonomously with the surrounding environment. By the mid-1990s, self-regulation was the de facto consensus in developmental psychology, with several of its academic champions like Edward Deci and Richard Ryan rapidly becoming the most cited and influential thought leaders in education. This was also a victory for the psychological discipline itself, as individualistic accounts of self-regulated cognition proved more amenable to applied interventions leading to measurable outcomes. There were, of course, debates about the exact nature of SRL, mostly revolving around the role of social and cultural determinants and influences but, overall, the basic conceptual and philosophical tenets of self-regulation were not contested. As digitisation and platformisation gathered pace in the late 2000s and early 2010s, self-regulation received another considerable boost, with the economic motifs of choice, speed and frictionless transactions between small suppliers and consumers going hand in hand with an equally breathless rhetoric of "participatory cultures" based on grassroots, intrinsically motivated engagement around shared interests and passions (Jenkins, 2009). Moreover, psychological self-regulation offered a ready theoretical rationale that seemed particularly well-aligned with notions of life-long learning and, it should not be underestimated, with a lucrative – often predatory – self-improvement industry that found fertile ground on the internet by supplying a wide array of products, services, and "content" aimed at assisting individuals in achieving personal growth and success.

Across all these unfolding trends, digital technology was regularly framed as a force for good that affords unprecedented levels of modularisation, while being attractive to self-regulating learners who can pick and mix educational opportunities, choosing how to participate according to their personal needs and preferences, in a typically consumptive fashion. In fact, it could be argued that platformisation has enabled forms of learning that resemble "content grazing": a widespread phenomenon in digital entertainment where people move from content to content without committing or completing (Perrotta et al., 2016). Recent evidence that supports such claims include a large-scale survey of online learning (Kross et al., 2021) which asked a demographically balanced sample of 2260 US citizens to describe the online learning resources they use on a regular basis. The findings are mostly relevant to the United States, but it is safe to surmise that similar results would be obtained in comparable contexts. The study reported widespread participation enabled by large adoption of broadband connectivity, with 93% of respondents learning online in some capacity, painting a picture of self-driven, yet ephemeral, engagement with a complex array of educational resources used by most participants (88%). The most-used platform by and large was YouTube, but the list also included MOOCs, Wikipedia, and online Q&A forums. This empirical work and the previous research that informed it (Kizilcec & Schneider, 2015; Kross et al., 2021) suggest that both formal (i.e., structured according to learning objectives and specific progression assumptions) and informal (i.e., organised more loosely around participating in communities of practice) modes of online learning are the result of self-directed consumptive behaviours. Formal online learners were overwhelmingly interested in STEM and data/computer science or programming, whereas people learning informally were drawn to video-tutorials to support pragmatic or passion-driven pursuits (planning a trip, or DIY). Based on these findings, it would appear that self-regulated learning is indeed the main form of learning across platform ecosystems. However, things are not quite so simple.

First, claims about the self-regulated nature of online learning must take into the account the inequalities that shape engagement with any form of technology. Like other forms of cultural, economic, and educational participation, opportunity is not dependent on choice alone, but is instead stratified according to socioeconomic factors, including gender, ethnicity and social class (Hoang et al., 2020; Rohs & Ganz, 2015). In this respect, it would be more accurate to say that for some privileged social groups online learning is a self-regulated affair motivated by a drive towards self-determination and autonomy. Second, and more germane to platformisation, we must distinguish between the motivations that might drive learning and the actual learning that occurs under specific sociotechnical conditions which were not designed to promote self-regulated human growth, but to extract value. Indeed, the empirical evidence in support of the self-regulation thesis only applies to the motivational side of the platformed learning equation, leaving the other half – the actual phenomenology of learning – in the dark. Motivated and self-regulating learners may autonomously make contact with platformed ecosystems, but what happens once they have been reeled in is a different matter altogether. Indeed, it could be argued that there is a tension between inherent motivations such as curiosity, the pursuit of novelty, and the quest for mastery, and the operational principles underpinning control and surveillance within platformed contexts. To better understand this contradiction, we need to look no further than the field of learning analytics, which emerged as a computational attempt to bridge the learning sciences and the affordances of digital platforms.

After a phase of initial, heady enthusiasm, the field found itself hampered by a tendency to use computational approaches in very narrow ways: to predict success or to provide datafied representations (dashboards) of educational performance, without any valuable theoretical insight into the conditions that co-determined those outcomes (Rogers et al., 2016). The consequence of this omission is twofold: an overreliance on palliative measures that target the symptoms (e.g., lack of motivation) rather than the root factors implicated in success or failure; and the uncritical acceptance of the implicit learning theories that inform the design of digital platforms. As Rogers, Gasevic, and Dawson put it: "the absence of explicit theory in predictive analytics research does not mean no theory" (p. 238). This notion of implicit theory chimes with a key sociological tenet: technical design is never based on a neutral "view from nowhere" but is informed by the sociocultural and disciplinary dispositions that precede it. Following this line of reasoning, the implicit learning theory of platformisation will most likely be a cybernetic one, philosophically attuned with the disciplinary tradition of algorithmic problem-solving that animates software design and concerned with mechanistic behaviour modification rather than aetiological analysis. Perhaps not behaviourist, but certainly "behaviouralist" in its emphasis on steering human action through the design of "choice architectures" (Kelkar, 2020). Thus, the philosophical tension between cybernetic self-regulation and the more humanistic educational notion of self-determination becomes apparent. Indeed, recent empirical evidence suggests that adaptive (algorithmic) technologies may actively undermine self-determination, especially when students' inability to regulate their learning is not addressed pedagogically but simply "resolved by the adaptive learning system taking over control and monitoring their progress" (Molenaar et al., 2021, p. 27). Given this risk, only a deliberate and theoretically informed design strategy will (hypothetically) steer platformed learning towards self-determination, because a platform logic reliant upon cybernetic feedback loops and datafied control mechanisms will work against autonomy if left unchecked.

An increasing recognition of these issues has prompted some within the learning analytics community to liken self-regulation in digital environments to a "wicked problem", caught up in an intractable tension between high-tech machinic precision and low-tech human open-endedness (Lodge et al., 2019). One the one side, a great deal of research and technological innovation pursues a granular and data-based analysis of self-regulation, correlating multiple sources of trace data including the non-verbal and non-conscious types, such as facial expressions and neurophysiological proxies. On the other side, it is abundantly clear that the relational nature of pedagogy is the single most important factor involved in the creation of appropriate conditions for self-driven behaviour and metacognitive awareness. The interesting aspect about the latter scenario is that

> Intervention strategies that target SRL-related processing do not need to be either comprehensive or precise. Simply prompting students to stop and consider whether the strategies they are using in their studies are effective, may be enough to get them to monitor their progress more closely and redirect their activity or employ different strategies. Much of the work in this instance can, therefore, be left to the intelligent student and not the "stupid" machine.
>
> *(Lodge et al., 2019, p. 51)*

The idea that effective self-regulated learning mainly relies on low-tech relational pedagogy and vague metacognitive prompting places the whole concept of learning through platforms under scrutiny. While it doesn't necessarily challenge the very notion of platformed learning, it does make one sceptical of the overhyped claims common in the edtech sector. It also raises the troubling thought that platformisation and automation might be a distraction from the actual educational challenge at stake: treating self-regulation as a sociopedagogical construct, rather than a matter of algorithmic measurement and optimisation.

As various forms of AI – generative or not – become embedded in educational platforms, issues of self-regulation are bound to become even more prevalent. This is because interactions between humans and AI can unpredictably swing between augmentation and disempowerment, with several supportive, offloading, and adversarial relationships already being observed or theorised (Guzdial et al., 2019; Jacob & Magerko, 2015; Jones, 2021; Köbis et al., 2021; Suh et al., 2021). AI can be, for instance, an active participant in a collaborative task, working alongside learners as a peer or assistant, often acting as a "psychological safety net" during the decisional process, allowing people to feel more comfortable taking risks and enhancing their metacognitive awareness. At the same time, AI can be an "enabler", encouraging unethical offloading decisions. As part of the latter scenario, AI and learners can become entangled in a dynamic of responsibility diffusion and fragmentation, with deflections, strategic delegations, and rationalisations which can undermine the integrity of the learning experience. Future efforts to promote self-regulated learning in platforms will need to consider critically how these relationships come into being and are negotiated in the authentic conditions of schooling and higher education.

The infrastructural curriculum of platformisation

The curriculum is a central notion in educational research, policy, and practice. Its primary meaning is "educational content", that is, knowledge that is worth knowing and which is propaedeutic to achieving a range of pro-social outcomes: economic prosperity, citizenship, and scientific discovery. This primary meaning informs direct or indirect policy provisions about teaching and learning. This definition may appear straightforward enough, but it conceals, like the tip of an iceberg, the sprawling complexity of a topic which, as Flinders and Thornton note (Flinders & Thornton, 2021, p. XI), resembles the "endless suburbs of a modern megalopolis. Its wide reach overlaps with every subject area; with cultural, political and economic trends; with philosophical concerns; and with social issues". One of the earliest publications on the topic was aptly titled "The Curriculum" and was authored in 1918 by Franklin Bobbitt, a University of Chicago professor and self-proclaimed pioneer who treated educational policy as a matter of scientific analysis and rational management – a design process inspired by the work of early behavioural psychologists like Thorndike (Eisner, 1967). This premise was vigorously rejected by John Dewey as he laid, approximately during the same period, the philosophical groundwork for a more critical and political reading of the curriculum. Famously, Dewey challenged purely managerial and normative approaches to the curriculum as encapsulating an unnatural and ideological denial of individual freedoms and lived experience (Dewey, 1938). With Dewey, the reproductive notion of the curriculum became apparent, that is, the fact that any attempt to organise knowledge and learning for educational purposes, no matter how purportedly neutral or disinterested, will reflect certain values about "what matters", and how social and economic relations should be arranged accordingly. This reproductive role of the curriculum became a topic of great sociological interest during the 1960s, as several critical interpretations began to challenge the conservative and constraining nature of social institutions.

One of the most influential among these critics was the French sociologist Pierre Bourdieu, who went on to develop an empirically grounded theory of social reproduction in education (Bourdieu & Passeron, 1990). Bourdieu introduced the notion of symbolic violence to capture the arbitrariness through which authority manifests itself and is legitimised in education. This educational imposition of meaning relies on the active concealment of the power relations that exist in society. It is not necessarily the result of deliberate ill will and operates more like a subtle, often unconscious cultural compulsion, which yet leaves room for a degree of autonomy: people can resist symbolic violence or can redefine its practical implications in their daily lives. As Bourdieu and Passeron put it: "To refuse this axiom, which states simultaneously the relative autonomy and the relative dependence of symbolic relations with respect to power relations, would amount to denying the possibility of a science of sociology" (Bourdieu & Passeron, 1990, p. 4). Such a sociological perspective greatly influenced, a few years later, the field of critical pedagogy (e.g., Giroux & Penna, 1979). Here, the concept of the "hidden curriculum" began to be used as a shorthand to describe the unseen consequences of the habitual arrangements of schooling, that is, the "day-to-day regularities" (Giroux & Penna, 1979, p. 22) that include epistemological but also material and spatial-temporal structures, as well as the disciplinary rules, the socialisation dynamics and the reward mechanisms that lead to the unquestioned acceptance of an ideological hegemony (Gramsci, 1971). More recently, these sociological discussions have prompted a long-overdue debate about decolonisation as a priority in curriculum studies – a historical necessity to valorise marginalised forms of knowledge that originated in suppressed indigenous cultures (Dei, 2010; Pinar, 2011).

In sum, there is a large body of sociological wisdom about the curriculum which can be drawn upon to examine the explicit educational promises and the hidden trappings of platformisation. Platforms can certainly "host" multiple educational curricula and can be very effective at regulating access to and provision of knowledge deemed worth having. This is possible because, as the previous chapter illustrated, platformisation is literally founded on a sort of epistemological agnosticism fuelled by an imaginary of limitless connection and mediation: the creation of interfaces where any form of content can be plugged in and amplified or empowered as a result, as long as it can be represented as data. Data representation, however, is not a neutral phenomenon but an act of selective translation which turns *some* people, *some* objects, and *some* relationships between them into enumerable abstractions, leaving out everything else. As a collection of theories and philosophical orientations, education is not new to this arbitrariness, because for a long time it has been grappling with a "crisis of representation", that is, the challenge to articulate and teach non-declarative and non-quantifiable forms of knowledge: the things that cannot be counted and which are not easily translated into standardised assessments of incremental growth (Eisner 1967). The rise of platformed education has not resolved this crisis but compounded it by widening the rift between quantifiable epistemologies, grounded in an individualistic understanding of learning as purely psychological and rational-economic, and more value-based, sociohistorical, and holistic perspectives on human development.

In addition, this "datafication of knowledge" imposes its own distinct epistemological requirements that operate as a hidden curriculum of platform literacy, where students are expected to develop competences that enable smooth coordination with sprawling platform ecosystems (Mertala, 2020). This hidden curriculum argument can be extended further by bridging the previously described sociological literature on the socially reproductive role of educational systems with recent contributions in infrastructure studies – forming a hybrid concept that could be termed the "infrastructural curriculum". As already introduced in Chapter 2, platformisation can be understood as a process of infrastructuring, which entails the establishment of sociotechnical arrangements (material and symbolic) that channel and regulate human activity. As Bowker and Star noted (Bowker & Star, 1999), the creation of infrastructures relies on the establishment of genre systems – typified communicative and cognitive templates that allow people to coordinate effectively within a sociotechnical network: patterns of behaviour, actions, or thoughts that are predictable and recognisable within a specific context, acting as shared expectations for how to behave in certain social situations or roles. These genre systems are therefore the "rules of the game" within infrastructures, which must be internalised if one wishes to participate. The educational implications are clear, as the establishment of genre systems is not always a tacit affair occurring in the background – a process of familiarisation through participation – but will often require explicit pedagogical action, understood here as Bourdieuan symbolic violence, to direct cognition and affect towards normative outcomes.

We can find evidence of this symbolic violence in the direct involvement of large technology companies in educational programme design, which has resulted in a complex and variegated landscape of accreditations, technological evangelism, instructional design, and branded learning materials: an infrastructural curriculum that seeks to mould "users" – teachers and learners – into platform workers familiar with the logics of software and able to navigate the market as potential employees and customers. Large technology companies have been advocating these self-referential infrastructural curricula for years, binding educational success and professional fulfilment to so-called 21st-century skills and their attendant tech-friendly epistemologies. These curricula have assimilated multiple forms of digital literacy, including the myriad "learning to code" initiatives that have proliferated at the intersection of corporate philanthropy and nation-level education governance since the early 2010s.

Recent scholarship on infrastructuring in global education further illuminates the nature of the infrastructural curriculum (Williamson et al., 2022). This research shows how large monopolistic providers like Amazon Web Services (AWS) control a global network of hardware, software, and interoperability protocols – a cloud-based regime that makes the creation of platform ecosystems in education possible. The establishment of this governing infrastructure involves multiple operations, with one in particular very relevant to the argument developed so far: the educational habituation to a positive discourse of the cloud, predicated upon the prospect of future personal success, and reliant on actual educational programmes. One of these programmes – AWS Educate – is used in more than 200 countries and territories and connects hundreds of thousands of students, educators and institutions, but it exists primarily as a satellite project revolving around AWS' core "cloud business", which focuses on data storage and remote analytics services sold to educational institutions. In short, AWS' role in education involves a cloud market that operates in the present, as a collection of business opportunities stemming from actual or perceived inefficiencies in educational governance. Extending out from this core business there is a long-term educational project – a roadmap leading to further adoption and expansion, towards personal futures shaped by desirable notions of individual fulfilment within a platformed economy.

44 Educating in platforms

In this protracted temporal dimension, AWS relies on an infrastructural curriculum, understood as a blend of explicit educational design and hidden reproductive logics, to establish its own brand of cloud-friendly cultural capital. Such a pursuit of infrastructural power through education and subjectification finds its utmost expression in the promotion of cloud degree programmes within universities, as AWS actively and self-assuredly intervenes in the creation of a new field of knowledge through faculty development and the embedding of cloud-specific learning objectives in higher education, such as the "4-year cloud degree pathway" sponsored in 2019 in collaboration with Northern Virginia Community College (NOVA), which allows higher education institutions to "meet employers' demand for tech talent while fulfilling their mission of expanding access to post-secondary education" (Busta, 2019, p. n.p.).

Platformed learning as topological dwelling

There is a strand of critical research that offers numerous insights into the "topological" nature of modern education (Lingard, 2022). Topology, in a general sense, refers to the study of the properties of space and time, and to how such properties are preserved or transformed in different environments and under multiple influences. The notion originated in mathematics, but it has been taken up in some philosophical circles. In this context, topology provided a framework to explore the "shape" or structure of experience without being tied to strict geometric or physical descriptions (Lury et al., 2012). This more philosophical understanding of topology is inextricably bound to digitisation, which has enabled environmental logics of control that do not reside in an enclosed space-time but are literally ambient and, as such, everywhere, with planes of sociality made and remade in multiple directions: "information is not transmitted between the environment, body and machines, but an entire ecology of information sensing is at play in the movement of transmission between channels" (Parisi, 2009, p. 188).

In plainer terms, this means that a great deal of cultural (and educational) interactions are now occurring on some sort of continuum rather than in distinct locations and times. As locations and times become blurred, a different notion acquires relevance: relation. The term "relation" certainly refers to how two or more entities are connected or associated, but also to something more dynamic and fluid that occurs "in medias res" – in the middle of things. In this more complex sense, relation is more like a motion across borders than a linear linkage between fixed and stable entities. This motion brings into being new identities and new forms of knowledge.

The notion of topological relation is interesting because it is non-deterministic. It accepts that platformisation can – despite its well-known problems – produce interesting and novel forms of educational policymaking and practice (Decuypere, 2021). In other words, a topological approach frames the digital and its attendant logics (infinite replicability, instantaneity, correlations on multiple and ever larger scales) as problems but also as opportunities affording potentially progressive forms of agency, and creating "new, possibly unsettling, political rationalities in education based on the cooperation between human and algorithmic cognition" (Gulson et al., 2022, p. 36). These contributions are important and innovative, but they have so far struggled to provide a clear answer to a key question: how do people actually learn in platformed environments? Luckily, there are ideas from this literature and from the broader disciplinary debates it takes inspiration from (post-structuralism, anthropology, human geography) which can be of assistance.

The key thesis to take forward and expand is that platformisation acts as a distinct form of space-time – a set of topological (geographical and chronological) arrangements superimposed on the pre-existing structures of education. As people (teachers, students, and other stakeholders) navigate this complex topology, they must learn to adapt and coordinate, mediating between the demands of the infrastructure and the human need to "make a home". Colin McFarlane's anthropological analysis of learning may be of assistance here (McFarlane, 2011). McFarlane understands learning as participation and belonging in urban infrastructures: a "heterogeneous engineering that demands a relational materialism" (ibid., p. 18). From this perspective, learning goes beyond formal knowledge acquisition and skill development, to encompass the political and lived-in dimension of geographical and symbolic space. In this expanded view, learning can be conceptualised as a flowing and dynamic assembling of affordances, resources, materials, histories – and, of course, forms of knowledge. Together, these features form a generative spatial grammar of learning that brings into view the experiences and contestations through which modern life is produced – a "learning to dwell" with others.

McFarlane's learning as dwelling borrows heavily from Tim Ingold's anthropology, in turn inspired by research on the ecological character of cognition as something that does not reside inside people's heads but happens everywhere, unfolding in the relationship between the whole organism and the surrounding environment (Ingold, 2022). Once immersed in this ecology, the mind – that unavoidable concept in any discussion about learning – emerges as a unified experience of consciousness and agency. The influence of Gregory Bateson's ecology is particularly strong here, especially his rejection of a hard boundary between human subjective experience and nature (Bateson, 2000). Bateson's famous example of the blind man with a cane is still very pertinent in this regard, acting as a powerful metaphor of the ecological entanglement between human experience, technology and the environment. Where does the blind person's experience end? Perhaps where the cognitive systems are located, in the brain? Or where the body meets the cane? Perhaps this boundary can be extended even further out, where the cane interacts with the environment as an extension of the blind person's perceptual system. All answers will be unsatisfactory, as the boundary (if one must be found) is constantly shifting, not least because the person is not static but dynamically moving in the surrounding space – not as an entirely individuated agent, but as an "organism plus environment" (Bateson, 2000, p. 423). In this scenario, learning becomes a sequence of practical enactments within intersecting ecologies, where minds-in-society operate following principles of apprehension, rather than representation – whatever we mean by representation: the cognitive representation of individual psychology or the mathematical representation of algorithmic abstraction. In contrast, apprehension is a holistic and organismic act of grasping complex phenomena, not by breaking them down in their constituent parts but by coming to terms with their incomputable nature and enfolding them within a unified – intuited – experience (Whitehead, 1967, 2020). Against this backdrop, learning-as-dwelling can be explained as a process of fitting and retrofitting (apprehending) reality to suit shifting ontological requirements; a constitutive act of worldmaking that makes life as we know it possible and is not entirely human, but human-plus-environment, which of course includes technology. As Ingold puts it (2022, p. 154) "worlds are made before they are lived in; or in other words, acts of dwelling are preceded by acts of worldmaking". In this sense, learning to dwell is a universal feature of the human (plus-environment) condition, realised in multiple intersecting ecologies – including the modern educational ecology being redefined by platformisation. Within the shifting and hybrid space-time of platformed education we can expect to observe forms of local dwelling which reflect the almost atavistic need to make a home. Learning to dwell in platformed educational ecosystems means engaging in individual and collective tactical enactments, often to find a "good enough" rather than optimal degree of coordination with infrastructures and their messy retinue of actors and sociotechnical arrangements: assessment regimes, datafication, curriculum contraction, international benchmarks, predictive modelling, marketisation and privatisation, and so forth. It manifests in daily routines, shortcuts, habitual movements, and deliberately disruptive omissions –the idiosyncratic actions that make life under increasingly oppressive and surveilling conditions bearable, and which arguably enable "other" forms of self-regulated and adaptive learning.

Clutterbuck, in her analysis of Queensland teachers becoming entangled with platformed logics, suggested something similar (Clutterbuck, 2022). Drawing on feminist and posthuman sensitivities (Barad, 2007; Haraway, 2004), she described a process of "diffraction", where education professionals navigating the gaps and interferences of platformed governance redefined their subjectivity and expertise accordingly. Thus, the platform "became an active contributor to education, blurring the lines between human and non-human participants and re-forming existing educational practitioners and their professional qualities" (Clutterbuck, 2022, p. 88).

Compared to the previous, more established educational perspectives – learning sciences and the sociology of education – this one can be described as a left-of-field anthropological orientation in need of further elaboration. As such, it seems fitting to explore it last as a plausible empirical proposal to take forward. More research is clearly needed on this expanded category of ecological learning as the very possibility of "dwelling" as a form of ontological and epistemological coordination with a digital infrastructure remains unclear. First Ingold and then Macfarlane developed their ideas with largely pre-digital contexts in mind. For them, learning to dwell is an adaptive, slow, and incremental process that rests upon not centuries but millennia of sedimented knowledge, manifesting as heterogeneous and improvised cultural practice. The extent to which this applies to modern platformed education remains an open question. After all, digital infrastructures are not only topological, but also "meteorological". They are certainly space-times but are also the air, the temperature, and light in which we increasingly live. The recent vernacular popularity of the term "gaslighting" comes to mind, as a strategy of ambient manipulation in which it is not much the space that changes but subtle environmental and affective aspects, which are modulated to steer behaviours and feelings towards specific outcomes.

What is more, this subtle influence is not aimless – it has directionality and a purpose. It is aligned with a hyper-individualistic and neoliberal worldview where people are treated as benefit-maximising agents seeking "biographical solutions of systematic contradictions" (Beck, 1992, p. 137). In the face of the growing complexity of society, it is possible that the participatory logics of platformisation are not encouraging liberating forms of "learning to dwell" but alienating ones, framing them as individualistic and competitive biographical projects. This "projectification" is indeed how many educational platforms operate, with individual learning and teaching practices framed as goal-oriented endeavours where outcomes are quantified, efforts tracked, and where time is channelled in the interest of accountability and self-promotion (Lewis & Decuypere, 2023). Educational participation is thus operationalised, often arbitrarily, as a collection of behavioural proxies and then moulded through structures of reward: achievements, badges, credits, and all the other signifiers of "project success". By partaking in these projects, teachers and students actively reproduce the data gaze of the platforms, shaping their personal identities according to a neoliberal discourse

48 Educating in platforms

of performativity. These are acts of deliberate "data submission" (Lewis & Hartong, 2022) where agents learn to live by attuning themselves to the datafied ecology of the digital infrastructure.

Conclusion

This chapter did something that, to my knowledge, has not yet been attempted in the nascent field of platform studies in education: a theoretical synthesis of "platformed learning" that brings together diverse disciplinary perspectives. The attempt began with possibly the most mainstream framework in educational psychology – self-regulated learning – to then consider seminal contributions in curriculum studies and the sociology of education, concluding with a more speculative examination of learning in anthropology and human geography. Together, these three perspectives represent interchangeable lenses to make sense of platformisation as an explicit educational project – one which is certainly underpinned by a vision of techno-political governance but cannot be reduced solely to it. People do learn and develop forms of tacit and codified knowledge within and across platforms. For adult learners, some of this learning is fuelled by a need for self-actualisation and self-regulation, which drives them towards platformed ecosystems and their promises of frictionless, plug-and-play education. However, the infrastructural logic of platforms may actively militate against self-regulation, as it prioritises cybernetic control over agency. Perhaps, self-regulated and participatory learning is more likely to occur informally, for instance on large social platforms like YouTube and TikTok, aided by the sheer size and heterogeneity of their user bases and the multimodal (mostly visual) nature of their content. However, upon closer inspection these communities are far from being havens of educational self-determination. They resemble more enclosures where people are simultaneously content creators and captive audiences, embroiled with proprietary infrastructures that reward free-floating engagement above all.

The second perspective brought to bear – curriculum studies – continued along the same path to show how educational theory can productively interact with infrastructure studies. As such, the notion of "infrastructural curriculum" may encourage a more critical discussion about the epistemological ramifications of platformisation, helping researchers, practitioners, and policymakers to recognise the tension between the explicit and tacit epistemologies that animate platformed education.

Finally, the third perspective offers a relatively novel reading on "learning to dwell" in platformed ecosystems. Once more, this is primarily an attempt to broaden the picture by drawing on disciplinary debates that regularly examine educational issues but are not normatively educational in their philosophical and political assumptions. At the very least, I hope this will illustrate that disciplines like developmental psychology and cognitive science do not hold exclusive ownership over the notion of platformed learning, and indeed, when it comes to complex (messy) sociotechnical phenomena, approaches versed in anthropological description and sociological interpretation can deliver refreshing alternatives.

References

Barad, K. (2007). *Meeting the universe halfway: Quantum physics and the entanglement of matter and meaning*. Duke University Press.

Bateson, G. (2000). *Steps to an ecology of mind: Collected essays in anthropology, psychiatry, evolution, and epistemology*. University of Chicago press.

Beck, U. (1992). *Risk society: Towards a new modernity*. Sage.

Boekaerts, M., & Niemivirta, M. (2000). Self-regulated learning: Finding a balance between learning goals and ego-protective goals. In M. Z. Boekaerts Moshe & P. R. Pintrich (Eds.), *Handbook of self-regulation* (pp. 417–450). Academic Press/Elsevier. https://doi.org/10.1016/B978-0-12-109890-2.X5027-6

Bourdieu, P., & Passeron, J.-C. (1990). *Reproduction in education, society and culture*. Sage.

Bowker, G. C., & Star, S. L. (1999). *Sorting things out: Classification and its consequences*. MIT Press.

Bronson, M. B., & Bronson, M. (2001). *Self-regulation in early childhood: Nature and nurture*. Guilford press.

Bruner, J. S. (1986). *Actual minds, possible worlds*. Harvard University Press.

Busta, H. (2019). *Partnership of the Year: A 4-year cloud degree pathway*. Retrieved October 13, 2023 from https://www.highereddive.com/news/cloud-degree-amazon-george-mason-nova-dive-awards/566275/

Clutterbuck, J. (2022). Data infrastructures and the governance of their accompanying narratives. *British Journal of Sociology of Education*, *43*(1), 120–139. https://doi.org/10.1080/01425692.2021.2003184

Deci, E. L., & Ryan, R. M. (2008). Self-determination theory: A macrotheory of human motivation, development, and health. *Canadian Psychology/Psychologie Canadienne*, *49*(3), 182. https://doi.org/10.1037/a0012801

Decuypere, M. (2021). The Topologies of Data Practices: A Methodological Introduction. *Journal of New Approaches in Educational Research*, *10*(1), 67–84. https://doi.org/10.7821/naer.2021.1.650

Dei, G. J. S. (2010). CHAPTER ONE: Rereading Fanon for His Pedagogy and Implications for Schooling and Education. *Counterpoints*, *368*, 1–27. Retrieved 14/11/2023, from https://www.jstor.org/stable/42980664

Dewey, J. (1938). *Experience and Education* Kappa Delta Pi.

Eisner, E. W. (1967). *Franklin Bobbitt and the "science" of curriculum making*. The University of Chicago Press.

Flinders, D. J., & Thornton, S. J. (2021). *The curriculum studies reader*. Routledge.

Giroux, H. A., & Penna, A. N. (1979). Social education in the classroom: The dynamics of the hidden curriculum. *Theory & Research in Social Education*, *7*(1), 21–42. https://doi.org/10.1080/00933104.1979.10506048

Gramsci, A. (1971). *Selections from the prison notebooks of Antonio Gramsci.* London, Lawrence & Wishart.

Gulson, K. N., Sellar, S., & Webb, P. T. (2022). *Algorithms of Education: How Datafication and Artificial Intelligence Shape Policy.* University of Minnesota Press. http://www.jstor.org/stable/10.5749/j.ctv2fzkpxp

Guzdial, M., Liao, N., Chen, J., Chen, S.-Y., Shah, S., Shah, V., Reno, J., Smith, G., & Riedl, M. O. (2019). Friend, Collaborator, Student, Manager: How Design of an AI-Driven Game Level Editor Affects Creators. Proceedings of the 2019 CHI conference on human factors in computing systems.

Haimovitz, K., & Dweck, C. S. (2017). The origins of children's growth and fixed mindsets: New research and a new proposal. *Child development, 88*(6), 1849–1859. https://doi.org/10.1111/cdev.12955

Haraway, D. J. (2004). *The Haraway Reader.* Psychology Press.

Hoang, L., Blank, G., & Quan-Haase, A. (2020). The winners and the losers of the platform economy: Who participates? *Information, Communication & Society, 23*(5), 681–700. https://doi.org/10.1080/1369118X.2020.1720771

Ingold, T. (2022). *The perception of the environment: Essays on livelihood, dwelling and skill.* Routledge.

Jacob, M., & Magerko, B. (2015). Interaction-based Authoring for Scalable Co-creative Agents – Proceedings of the Sixth International Conference on Computational Creativity June 2015. *ICCC*, 236–243. https://computationalcreativity.net/iccc2015/proceedings/10_3Jacob.pdf

Jenkins, H. (2009). *Confronting the challenges of participatory culture: Media education for the 21st century.* The MIT press.

Jones, R. H. (2021). The text is reading you: Teaching language in the age of the algorithm. *Linguistics and Education, 62.* https://doi.org/10.1016/j.linged.2019.100750

Kelkar, S. (2020). *Are Surveillance Capitalists Behaviorists? No. Does It Matter? Maybe.* Retrieved 6/10/2023 from https://culturedigitally.org/2020/12/are-surveillance-capitalists-behaviorists-no-does-it-matter-maybe/

Kizilcec, R. F., & Schneider, E. (2015). Motivation as a lens to understand online learners: Toward data-driven design with the OLEI scale. *ACM Transactions on Computer-Human Interaction (TOCHI), 22*(2), 1–24. https://doi.org/10.1145/2699735

Köbis, N., Bonnefon, J.-F., & Rahwan, I. (2021). Bad Machines Corrupt Good Morals. *Nature Human Behaviour, 5*(6), 679–685. https://doi.org/10.1038/s41562-021-01128-2

Kross, S., Hargittai, E., & Redmiles, E. M. (2021). Characterizing the online learning landscape: What and how people learn online. *Proceedings of the ACM on Human-Computer Interaction, 5*(CSCW1), 1–19.

Lewis, S., & Decuypere, M. (2023). 'Out of time': Constructing teacher professionality as a perpetual project on the eTwinning digital platform. *Tertium Comparationis, 29*(1), 22–47. https://doi.org/10.31244/tc.2023.01.02

Lewis, S., & Hartong, S. (2022). New shadow professionals and infrastructures around the datafied school: Topological thinking as an analytical device. *European Educational Research Journal, 21*(6), 946–960. https://doi.org/10.1177/14749041211007496

Lingard, B. (2022). Relations and locations: New topological spatio-temporalities in education. *European Educational Research Journal*, *21*(6), 983–993. https://doi.org/10.1177/14749041221076323

Lodge, J. M., Panadero, E., Broadbent, J., & De Barba, P. G. (2019). Supporting self-regulated learning with learning analytics. In J. Lodge, J. Cooney Horvath, & L. Corrin (Eds.), *Learning analytics in the classroom: Translating learning analytics research for teachers* (pp. 45–55). Routledge.

Lury, C., Parisi, L., & Terranova, T. (2012). Introduction: The Becoming Topological of Culture. *Theory, culture & society*, *29*(4–5), 3–35. https://doi.org/10.1177/0263276412454552

McFarlane, C. (2011). *Learning the City: Knowledge and Translocal Assemblage*. Wiley.

Mertala, P. (2020). Data (il)literacy education as a hidden curriculum of the datafication of education. *Journal of Media Literacy Education*, *12*(3), 30–42. https://doi.org/10.23860/JMLE-2020-12-3-4

Molenaar, I., Horvers, A., & Baker, R. S. (2021). What can moment-by-moment learning curves tell about students' self-regulated learning? *Learning and Instruction*, *72*, 101206. https://doi.org/10.1016/j.learninstruc.2019.05.003

Parisi, L. (2009). Technoecologies of sensation. In B. Herzogenrath (Ed.), *Deleuze/Guattari & Ecology* (pp. 182–199). Palgrave Schol.

Perrotta, C., Czerniewicz, L., & Beetham, H. (2016). The rise of the video-recorder teacher: The sociomaterial construction of an educational actor. *British Journal of Sociology of Education*, *37*(8), 1251–1267. https://doi.org/10.1080/01425692.2015.1044068

Piaget, J. (2002). *Judgement and reasoning in the child*. Routledge.

Pinar, W. (2011). *The character of curriculum studies: Bildung, currere, and the recurring question of the subject*. Springer.

Pintrich, P. R., & Zusho, A. (2007). Student Motivation and Self-Regulated Learning in the College Classroom. In R. P. Perry & J. C. Smart (Eds.), *The Scholarship of Teaching and Learning in Higher Education: An Evidence-Based Perspective* (pp. 731–810). Springer Netherlands. https://doi.org/10.1007/1-4020-5742-3_16

Rogers, T., Gašević, D., & Dawson, S. (2016). Learning analytics and the imperative for theory driven research. In C. Haythornthwaite, R. Andrews, J. Fransman, & E. Meyers (Eds.), *The SAGE Handbook of E-Learning Research* (pp. 232–250).

Rohs, M., & Ganz, M. (2015). MOOCs and the claim of education for all: A disillusion by empirical data. *International review of research in open and distributed learning*, *16*(6), 1–19. https://doi.org/10.19173/irrodl.v16i6.2033

Suh, M., Youngblom, E., Terry, M., & Cai, C. J. (2021). AI as social glue: Uncovering the roles of deep generative AI during social music composition. Proceedings of the 2021 CHI conference on human factors in computing systems,

Von Glasersfeld, E. (2013). *Radical constructivism*. Routledge.

Vygotsky, L. S., & Cole, M. (1978). *Mind in society: Development of higher psychological processes*. Harvard University Press.

Whitehead, A. N. (1967). *Aims of education*. Simon and Schuster.

Whitehead, A. N. (2020). *Whitehead's The Function of Reason*. Lindhardt og Ringhof.

Wiener, N. (1961/2019). *Cybernetics or Control and Communication in the Animal and the Machine – Reissue Of The 1961 Second Edition.* MIT press.

Williamson, B., Gulson, K. N., Perrotta, C., & Witzenberger, K. (2022). Amazon and the new global connective architectures of education governance. *Harvard Educational Review*, *92*(2), 231–256. https://doi.org/10.17763/1943-5045-92.2.231

4

THE UNREASONABLE AI OF PLATFORMISATION

The relationship between AI, automation, and platformisation

There is a very close relationship between platformisation and the growth of Artificial Intelligence (AI). This chapter will examine this relationship and consider the educational ramifications. Before doing so, however, it is important to lay out some historical background which will help clarify the specific form of AI considered here. Despite being described as one of the most promising – and intimidating – technological trends of the 21st century, AI has a long and checkered history that dates to the 1950s at least, with a well-documented pattern of hype followed by backlash. If we arbitrarily consider 1950 – when Alan Turing introduced his eponymous test to distinguish between an artificial and human agent – as the birth year of modern AI, then the first backlash took place shortly thereafter following the struggles of "symbolic AI", which indeed emerged from Turing's seminal work in mathematical logic. The very first example of symbolic AI – aptly named Logic Theorist – was a program developed in 1956 by three of the founding figures of the field: Allen Newell, Herbert Simon and Cliff Shaw (Newell & Simon, 1956). The program was hand-simulated on 3x5 cards and designed to act like a mathematician, using branching deductive trees and heuristics (rules of thumb) to prove theorems.

Two years later, in 1958, Frank Rosenblatt, a research psychologist at Cornell Aeronautical Laboratory in Buffalo, New York, proved that a machine – a "perceptron" – could be designed to learn and make decisions by processing information much like a human neuron. The perceptron experiment was not based on symbolic AI but was rooted in a different paradigm

DOI: 10.4324/9781003099826-4

54 The unreasonable AI of platformisation

known as connectionism, which seeks to model information processing in a manner inspired by neural networks in biological brains. The experiment involved feeding the perceptron apparatus – a camera connected to an array of electrical resistors – inputs (like images or numbers), each associated with a specific weight (importance). The perceptron would sum up these weighted inputs, and, if the total surpassed a certain threshold, it would produce an output (a decision). The fascinating part is that the perceptron could learn from its mistakes: if it made an incorrect decision, the weights of the inputs would be adjusted to make the future decisions more accurate. In other words, the perceptron was capable of basic learning through adjusting its weights based on errors, similar to how humans learn from mistakes. The enthusiasm caused by Rosenblatt's successful demonstration proved, however, fleeting.

Only 11 years later, in 1969, Marvin Minsky and Seymour Papert published their famous book *Perceptrons*, which compellingly proved that the apparatus was structurally unable to recognise certain shape configurations and could not be trained to do so (Minsky & Papert, 1969). The impact on the nascent field of AI was dramatic, and it effectively put a stop to all research. Activity timidly resumed several years later following the development of "expert systems" in the late 1970s and 1980s. These systems sought to replicate human experts by applying a procedural logic largely based on if/then conditional branching, which was then used to provide guidance in the context of specific, hand-crafted knowledge domains. This form of AI was a direct evolution of the symbolic approach, building upon several ideas about mental representation and problem-solving which were ahead of their time when Logic Theorist introduced them nearly 30 years before (Gugerty, 2006). Expert systems also faltered, and this led to another "AI winter" which lasted approximately another decade, until the current enthusiasm for machine learning began to emerge in the mid-1990s. This shift marked a resurgence of the connectionist approach, and the beginning of the current era of AI (Christian, 2020).

During this period, influential computer scientists like Yann Lecun, Yoshua Bengio, and Richard Sutton laid the foundations for understanding the potential of neural networks for image recognition, and for how artificial agents can learn optimal behaviours through reward policies. The shortcomings of the original Perceptron were overcome through more complex and multilayered algorithmic design, but the most significant enabler of this AI renaissance was the rise of so-called big data, that is, the unprecedented levels of digitisation and large-scale quantification brought about by the internet at the end of the 1990s and the early 2000s. During these years, platformisation rapidly became the dominant paradigm in the digital economy, establishing the socioeconomic conditions that made AI finally viable after several false starts. Indeed, there is no AI – at least as we understand it nowadays (predictive modelling, automated decision-making and generative foundation models) – without platforms, because they extract the essential training material (data) and are the main sites of implementation of the resulting applications. We give data, which is then used to develop AI models, all without ever leaving a constantly growing ecosystem of interconnected platforms. We can find several examples of cutting-edge AI in this ecosystem: smart search algorithms tackling ever-growing magnitudes of information at a super-human scale, behaviour prediction in multiple commercial and non-commercial applications (including, of course, education), and the automation of human communicative and cognitive functions. Much has already been written about AI and the planetary data infrastructures that buttress it, and we are now beginning to comprehend the unique – surreal even – epistemological ramifications. I am referring to how the vagaries of human participation in a largely artificial context of platformed sociality and economics have come to define what counts as valuable and reliable knowledge.

The seven pieces of the current AI jigsaw

This section offers a brief synoptic summary of the main defining features of the contemporary approach to artificial intelligence. It is a partial and subjective synthesis of ideas and makes no claims of being exhaustive, but it does provide a helpful compass for the remainder of the chapter, paving the way for the "unreasonableness" argument introduced in the next section.

1. *Extraction*: contemporary AI operates on a foundational principle of extraction, which is evident in various aspects of its development, production, and functionality (Crawford, 2021). Initially, AI systems rely heavily on the extraction of physical materials from the Earth, essential for building the hardware on which these systems run. Additionally, the operation and training of AI involve extensive data extraction. This begins with the collection of vast amounts of data from the internet to train the system, followed by the continuous acquisition of data generated through the regular use of AI applications.
2. *Many diverse families*: AI is often treated as a monolithic phenomenon. A more accurate approach might be to examine specific AI subsets and families and their concrete applications. Consider robotic locomotion, an AI branch evolving from Zero Motion Point (ZMP) algorithms, which govern motion, position, and equilibrium in practical settings. Machine learning and deep learning belong to another subset, where algorithmic methods are used to discern data patterns and forecast outcomes for new data.

These methods might range from basic statistical techniques like linear regression, plotting a line in two-dimensional space to predict one variable based on another, to intricate multilayered neural networks that mimic aspects of the human brain. These different "families" of AI are often deployed alongside each other, depending on the application scenario. For instance, while ZMP algorithms and deep learning operate on different principles, they can interact in advanced robotics applications, with deep learning used to improve the perception and decision-making capabilities of a robot, which in turn can enhance the effectiveness of ZMP-based control algorithms.

3. *Learning from data*: most AI algorithms "learn" by interacting with training datasets. This learning begins, unsurprisingly perhaps, with human agents – model architects and data scientists – assembling training sets of observations, consisting of inputs and outputs associated with a phenomenon or collection of phenomena. The training sets are then fed to a learning algorithm: a software artefact where code and maths become intimately interwoven. The algorithm gradually learns how to differentiate between different features of the data, say, images of cats and dogs, to then apply that discerning ability to unseen data instances: presented with a new image, the trained algorithm can determine whether it is a cat, a dog or neither. This learning process is based on an iterative approximation that comes to an end when the human agents, according to certain criteria (quantitative and qualitative), decide that satisfactory results have been obtained. Learning from data begins during model development but it often continues during model implementation, as most models require constant tweaking through further training to maintain performance and to avoid gross misclassifications when deployed intensively in the wild. However, several "generative" language models emerged in the late 2010s and early 2020s, such as Generative Pre-Trained Transformer (GPT), are able to adapt and generalise to unseen scenarios with great ease, only requiring little new training (few-shots training) and sometimes without needing new training at all (zero-shot training). This semblance of generality has given these models an aura of multipurpose, quasi-human intelligence that obfuscates a key structural condition that remains relevant despite generative AI's great strides in the early 2020s: computational tractability.

4. *Computational tractability*: this concept refers to AI systems' capacity being limited in their ability to solve a problem in a reasonable amount of time and with feasible resource requirements. Computational tractability involves assessing whether a given task can be completed efficiently with existing computational methods and hardware and is crucial in determining the practicality and efficiency of algorithms and computational

processes, especially when dealing with large datasets or complex calculations. This concept highlights a limitation in AI: it still struggles with data that is ambiguous, highly subjective, or not easily quantifiable, such as complex human emotions or abstract concepts.

5. *Supervised, unsupervised and reinforced*: the process of learning from data can occur in three ways, which together cover the entire terrain of contemporary AI. In supervised learning, the algorithm learns from a dataset which has been labelled and curated in advance. In this scenario, there is a human-defined framework that determines how the model is expected to behave when it encounters never-seen-before instances. In an unsupervised learning scenario, the model learns from unlabelled data, "discovering" patterns and data representations without any predefined criteria. In a reinforcement scenario, the model also learns unsupervised, but it does so according to a reward policy, which determines desirable or "win" states vs. undesirable or "lose" states

6. *Trade-offs*: optimal models typically align moderately with the data they have been trained on, as models with a perfect fit may yield inaccurate predictions and classifications. A trade-off always takes place when choosing between a detailed yet potentially cluttered data representation and a simpler, more predictive but possibly incomplete model: something potentially valuable about the phenomenon of interest is sacrificed in the interest of performance.

7. *Humans in the loop*: the development of AI models is an iterative and social process that lets in the computational preferences of model architects and requires constant human oversight. The former "creep in" through the domain knowledge assumptions and selective conventions (social, statistical, and computational) that help transform unstructured collections of numbers, text, and visual data into computable material. The latter is mobilised in often problematic ways, for instance in the form of a sprawling global network of algorithmic workers who manually annotate datasets during the training phase, or who oversee content while remaining largely unnoticed in the background (Tubaro et al., 2020). This need for human moderation and labelling is, however, rarely acknowledged in public, as it undermines the marketing rhetoric of seamlessness and superhuman ability surrounding AI, that is, the "fauxtomation" wilfully perpetuated by large economic interests (Taylor, 2018).

The unreasonableness of AI

At the heart of the current enthusiasm for AI lies the profoundly unwarranted tenet that our past technological lives, that is, our multiple entanglements with devices and software over time, represent a reasonable proxy that can inform the development of predictive systems and automated agents.

The word "reasonable" is key here and it should not be confused with "rational". The data collected from digital platforms, social media, smart devices, and the Internet of Things (IoT) are very much rational proxies with proven predictive power when aggregated at scale. The real question is whether the knowledge extracted from these technological systems is a sound – indeed reasonable – representation of our lived experience, upon which we can build governance systems and autonomous "generative" agents that have real and life-changing impacts. I use the concept of reason here in a Whiteheadian sense (Stengers, 2011), as a process not limited to abstracting and generalising from antecedent states, but which is instead capable of "speculation" following an upward motion from experience: "what distinguishes men from the animals, some humans from other humans, is the inclusion in their natures, waveringly and dimly, of a disturbing element, which is the flight after the unattainable" (Whitehead, 2020, p. 65).

This may seem like an obscurantist position that clings to a vague notion of human exceptionalism, in the face of mounting evidence that even the most ineffable components of intelligence can now – or will soon – be computationally modelled. Some forms of reinforcement learning, for example, can now incorporate in their reward policies a generalist quest for novelty and intellectual curiosity. Despite these advancements, the argument still stands, since it is not concerned with the ability of models to adapt to unexpected scenarios (i.e., what AI innovation pursues) but about the human inclination to be "more" than what our present or past conditions would warrant. This is what "speculative reason" means and is very much related to what Hannah Arendt called "enlarged mentality": the ability to make present to ourselves what was absent in our experience and in the historical data (Arendt, 1998). There is, after all, plentiful evidence that people, when included in certain categories based on their past behaviours, may resist. Indeed, these are the "looping effects" described by Ian Hacking: the overuse of synthetic and arbitrary elements of differentiation may lead to scenarios where people react negatively to being classified: "what was known about people of a kind may become false because people of that kind have changed in virtue of what they believe about themselves" (Hacking, 1999, p. 34). This issue speaks loudly to the "alignment problem" of AI: the challenge of ensuring that AI systems reflect human values and democratic principles. As the best-selling author Brian Christian noted in his titular book:

> This is the delicacy of our present moment. Our digital butlers are watching closely. They see our private as well as our public lives, our best and worst selves, without necessarily knowing which is which or making a distinction at all. They by and large reside in a kind of uncanny valley of sophistication: able to infer sophisticated models of our desires from our

behavior, but unable to be taught, and disinclined to cooperate. They're thinking hard about what we are going to do next, about how they might make their next commission, but they don't seem to understand what we want, much less who we hope to become.

(Christian, 2020, pp. 328–329)

AI's inability to reproduce this speculative function of reason (hoping to be more than what we are) is the result of a structural limitation: its dependency on "detections" of antecedent states – "signifiers whose referent is no longer a human subject but a cluster of correlations" (Bolin & Andersson Schwarz, 2015, p. 4). The rationale that justifies this epistemological error is based on an inductivist fantasy of "framelessness" – a pathology, according to Andrejevic (2020) – that leads some to believe there can be a fully formed and unfettered 1:1 digital informational trove, where the entirety (without frames or filters) of human experience has been captured, and which is ready to be lifted from platformed ecosystems. Moreover, such frameless data trove is construed as a phenomenon that exceeds the human ability to process it and understand it. Thus, its very existence justifies the offloading of sense-making unto the superior computational capabilities of machines. The fantasy of 1:1 data does not do away with the human need to impose frames, but simply replaces a human inferencing with a stochastic one, which is not more effective or purer but just as likely to be poisoned by biases: epistemic preferences and reasoning dispositions, but also messier things like social disadvantage and multiple forms of inequality crystallised in our social structures. Indeed, it could not be any different because these issues are not transient or anomalous aspects – blips in the system – but endemic features of participation in platformed contexts. Indeed, after the the early enthusiasm for the democratising power of platforms, research began to show that class, race, gender, and the associated inequalities were mirrored in their genesis and subsequent development. Examples include the birth of Facebook in the exclusive milieu of Harvard university and the subsequent "white flight" from the old competitor MySpace (Boyd, 2011), the overwhelming presence of white male discourse on social media and its unsavoury sexist ramifications (Massanari, 2017), and the fact that flexible online learning opportunities are for the most a privilege limited to those in the global north (Rohs & Ganz, 2015). The response to these problems of platform monoculturalism, toxicity, and bias has been singular: to collect ever larger quantities of data.

Some readers may recall the breathless corporate rhetoric of "data as the new oil" during the mid-2000s (Palmer, 2006), which was utterly discredited when it became clear that digital data do not emerge in a void, but from a milieu of sociotechnical conditions. Unlike oil, data are created at the very point of extraction, and then remade through several transformative cycles.

During these cycles, sociocultural biases creep in through the algorithmic operations that turn amorphous aggregations of numbers, text, and visual noise into computationally usable material. The risk intrinsic in this transformation is the loss of contextual nuance or, more pertinent to the point being made here, the wilful obfuscation of the social and cultural factors that can explain patterns as something else – or more – than what can be inferred from the data alone. This is, to reiterate, what "unreasonableness" means in this discussion: an act of epistemological and intellectual erasure renders AI unreasonable.

This erasure can be found in the many educational applications of predictive modelling, as Madisson Whitman (Whitman, 2020) showed in her ethnographic study at a large public university in the United States, where computational experts actively intervened in the sorting of student data, creating a discursive uncoupling between fixed demographic "attributes" that could not be changed, and actionable "behaviours" which were not fixed and could therefore be nudged towards desirable outcomes. However, the fixedness that separated attributes from behaviours was not a self-evident criterion, but the result of an ethical-political determination that the algorithmic process had contributed to conceal, but which was still very much active behind the scenes. Data administrators would decide that certain markers of identity and social standing were off limits (fixed) and could not be nudged. This was followed by an equally arbitrary and contingent determination about what counted as a behaviour, according to an impressionistic heuristic of choice: if a data point (e.g., accessing the campus Wi-Fi, or a card-swiping to enter the library), was viewed as the result of individual agency and free will, even when closer inspection and a degree of contextual awareness would invite caution, it would be categorised as a behaviour and it would be deemed amenable to algorithmic nudging. The logic that underpins the classification of a student in Whitman's research echoes familiar debates in public health, where certain lifestyles and choices (e.g., healthy eating) are construed in terms of individual responsibility for purely ideological reasons. In this particular case study, the process was not as blatantly ideological and it was indeed animated by a genuine commitment to fairness; nonetheless, Whitman notes that it was equally the result of a particular imaginary that sought to establish a "regime of self-regulation" (p. 10), which arbitrarily framed students as free agents in control of their educational destinies.

The unreasonableness of AI is ultimately a form of "symbolic violence" – a concept already introduced in Chapter 3 to explain the arbitrary impositions of meaning that conceal the power relations in society (Bourdieu & Passeron, 1990). Unsurprisingly, symbolic violence is often harmful. Examples of the harmful impacts resulting from digital systems of governance are plentiful:

The unreasonable AI of platformisation **61**

the structural difficulty of image classifiers to recognise non-white and non-male features, automated employment advertising displaying fewer high-paying positions aimed at women, the development of creditworthiness criteria which excluded low-income and ethnically diverse populations, and racial bias in predictive policing (Barocas & Selbst, 2016; Buolamwini & Gebru, 2018; Datta et al., 2014; Eubanks, 2018; Goel et al., 2016). In all these examples, previous patterns of behaviour, automatically recorded and then classified according to questionable normative standards, determined actual barriers to opportunity or were downright damaging. In education, algorithmic harm became a topic of mainstream interest in 2020, when Ofqual, the body regulating qualifications and exams in the UK, created a "grades standardisation algorithm" for exams sat by all students at ages 16 and 18 – the General Certificate of Secondary Education (GCSE) and the A Levels exam. The model was, however, biased, as it consistently assigned lower grades to students from public schools (Satariano, 2020).

In several of the instances listed above, harms materialised even when no actual personal data were provided, but simply because AI models now operate on the basis of shared population characteristics. The assumption that what is effective for a group is equally effective for another group because they share certain population characteristics is an arbitrary determination that unreasonably brackets the social ecologies in which people live, as well as their individual existential dispositions. In short, a vast body of knowledge about personal and social contexts disappears into these systems, while harmful classifications remain and are endowed with additional force. Turning our attention to these potentially life-changing erasures serves as a reminder that platformisation is not about specific software environments and their capabilities, but a far-reaching change in how social life is organised through and around technology. Indeed, we are already at a point where opaque AI systems could plausibly replace more ethical and responsible forms of human decision-making in several contexts. An alternative scenario is one where such systems complement rather than replace human decisions; where they are not designed to be opaque but are always clear about the motives and identities of their creators; and where zero-sum competitive markets – when companies invest in AI to outdo each other rather than to pursue the public good – are avoided. Frank Pasquale turned these pragmatic ethical concerns into "new laws of robotics" (Pasquale, 2020) as a nod to the old laws proposed by the science fiction writer Isaac Asimov (a robot must prioritise avoiding harm to humans, obey their commands unless it conflicts with the first law, and safeguard its own existence without violating the first two laws). I will return to Pasquale's laws in the conclusion, but first I wish to expand on the "unreasonableness" assumption by examining two implications: the first relates to responsibility and delegation, framed as topics of great educational importance; the second has to do with the interpretability of AI's internal operations.

Unreasonable AI and educational responsibility

The argument developed in the previous section is that the current AI paradigm is unreasonable because of three structural flaws: (a) the unsound knowledge platformed systems depend upon (internet data), (b) the opacity of the knowledge they produce through their outputs, and (c) the political and practical knowledge they impair when they (partly or completely) take over decisional processes. All these problems deserve our attention, but the last one is perhaps the most consequential from an educational perspective. At its core lies a key problem: responsibility.

Responsibility is a central, often overlooked concept in education. The very foundation of this institution is based on a collective act of delegation, as elements of upbringing historically transitioned from the household to informal and formal structures of knowledge transmission and behaviour control. This transition was, of course, grounded in a great deal of common-sense wisdom about the role of communities, social institutions, and relevant "others" in the cognitive and moral development of young ones, and it was supported by a century of psychological and sociological progress showing that humans seek and cherish shared responsibility because it may increase the collective good. At the very centre of this process of collective delegation was the educator – the teacher, the tutor, the professor, and so forth – engaged in relational and embodied pedagogical practice, which manifests in multiple forms during the life course, is sustained by an evolutionary and biological substratum, and is deeply embedded in linguistic and cultural traditions – not necessarily Western ones.

From this rich tradition stems a deontological view of education, understood as a site of great collective and individual (professional) responsibility. Dewey (1930) examined this educational responsibility extensively in his philosophy and identified two overarching aims of education: (1) emancipation: to create environments where young people have an opportunity to break away from the "mental habitudes" (p. 25) they acquired elsewhere; (2) to prepare for the future, not by placing young people on a "waiting list" (p. 58) but by valorising their present experiential conditions. These aims are noble but also meaningless if pursued irrespective of the specific social conditions of education. They must be translated in the sphere of pedagogical practice as a distinct form of educational responsibility connected with goal-oriented action. Like farmers, educators are individuals pragmatically engaged in producing an outcome. Both perform certain actions daily, which allow for a degree of discretion but are never arbitrary because they are

The unreasonable AI of platformisation   **63**

shaped by the opportunities and constraints of the environment: seasons, pests, fires for the former, and human and social variance for the latter. Understanding the contextual conditions in which action occurs is therefore a key dimension of responsibility. Neglecting these conditions may lead to a fallacious and possibly harmful pursuit of a "noble" aim.

> Aims mean acceptance of responsibility for the observations, anticipations, and arrangements required in carrying on a function—whether farming or educating. Any aim is of value so far as it assists observation, choice, and planning in carrying on activity from moment to moment and hour to hour; if it gets in the way of the individual's own common sense (as it will surely do if imposed from without or accepted on authority) it does harm.
>
> *(Dewey, 1930, p. 112)*

The farming analogy may appear naïve to the cynic's eye, but in fact adds a material and "down to earth" dimension to the problem of educational responsibility, configuring it as a reasonable endeavour grounded in space, time and relationships. The parallels with the previous discussion, where the unreasonableness of AI was introduced, are clear. What happens when educators place their trust in unreasonable systems, where human and social variance has been expunged? The answer, echoing Dewey, is that harms may materialise. In a best-case scenario, automated classifications may prove to be erroneous or biased and thus require constant oversight; in a worst-case scenario, teachers have become unable to exercise judgment, as multiple automated systems operate synchronously behind the scenes impacting upon the sphere of professional work and leading to a fragmentation of responsibility. Drawing on research on the ethics of innovation (van de Poel & Sand, 2021), we can plausibly hypothesise the emergence of the following deficits in contexts where educational decisions can be fully or partly delegated to machines:

1. accountability deficits: no one can provide a rationale or take responsibility for an educational decision.
2. culpability deficits: no one can be held morally responsible for an educational harm.
3. compensation deficits: no one is responsible for restorative measures to an educational harm caused by an automated system, financial or otherwise.
4. Obligation deficits: no one is responsible to ensure that future uses of a platformed system reflect sound educational values.
5. virtue deficit: no one is responsible to foster a culture of responsibility for the action of a platformed system in education.

The risk of responsibility deficits is entwined with another challenge: the interpretability of algorithmic behaviour and outcomes, officially recognised in the public discourse and in corporate sectors as one of the main barriers to the social acceptance of artificial intelligence. It is indeed self-evident that transparent and readily available disclosure about the assumptions that underpin a decision is a necessary condition to avoid a problematic and potentially harmful delegation of responsibility.

Interpreting unreasonable AI

The interpretability of deep learning, one of the most opaque forms of non-representational AI where models learn to recognise patterns and relationships directly from data, without requiring predefined structures, can be increased by building semantic dictionaries and visualising the relationships between human-defined concepts and the model's internal information processing operations (Olah et al., 2018; Zhang & Zhu, 2018). Semantic dictionaries are collections of words or terms presented alongside their corresponding meanings or semantic representations. By mapping the internal operations of a neural network to semantically meaningful terms, it is possible to gain an insight into the specific features or concepts the network is detecting. These procedures can help bridge the gap between the abstract numerical representations of deep learning and meaningful and relatively accessible concepts that can be expressed through language.

Whilst I do not dispute the importance of these efforts, they might lead to an overly technicist preoccupation with the legibility of individual algorithmic operations, at the expense of the overarching logics: the forms of stochastic and fallacy-prone decisional processes that these methods aim to replicate. Deep learning, in particular, is based on a rather primitive notion of intelligence better described as a suboptimal process of abstraction informed by prior probability. This process is hamstrung by its reliance on a set of trade-offs that make an optimal use of all available information impossible: "one can view artificial intelligence as a quest to find shortcuts: ways of (…) sacrificing some optimality or generality while preserving enough to get high performance in the actual domains of interest" (Bostrom, 2014, p. 9).

While Bostrom and many other "AI champions" frame this pursuit of efficiency in largely positive terms, I prefer to see it as a reminder that humans behave in similar ways, not through the explicit mathematical formalisms of algorithmic design but through embodied interaction with an uncertain environment (Lakoff, 2012). Therefore, AI recreates rather primitive decisional logics that are as problematic in machines as they are in humans, reproducing the same issues and biases of human judgement without the moderating and filtering functions of embodied social discourse and contextual adaptability. With this caveat in mind, the only revelation to be gained by opening the black box of AI is that its inner workings are based on just as much guesswork as the inner workings of human cognition and communication, and that such inherent shortcoming is overcome in the most unimaginative way possible: through more data collection and by deploying an unprecedented degree of computational muscle, that is, brute forcing its way to accuracy and reliability. This echoes Ananny and Crawford's argument that that there may be no revelatory truth worth excavating from AI infrastructure after all, and therefore we would better off redirecting our attention to relations and dialecticism: the political-economic contestations and the social enactments that surround computational design and usage (Ananny & Crawford, 2018).

Until now, critical commentary in algorithm and data studies has mostly developed from a recognition of the power exercised through classifications and measurement: "what the categories are, what belongs in a category, and who decides how to implement these categories in practice, are all powerful assertions about how things are and are supposed to be" (cf. Bowker & Star, 1999; Gillespie, 2014, p. 171). The potential impact of AI on human agency requires us to apply the same critical lens to another order of phenomena: the partial and error-prone inference logics that underpin current forms of computational intelligence. Bringing into view these key aspects of computation might help us cast a critical light on the uncertainty that permeates AI, from the ways in which neural activations operate automatically, to the biases that creep in when models are being trained. Heterogeneity is the only ever-present constant here: it is always possible to pick alternative models because, from a purely probabilistic perspective, there are always multiple reasonable courses of action, and the relationship between models and outcomes (classifications and predictions) is constantly updating as new observations become available.

Acknowledging and valorising this heterogeneity may be the key to reframe in more reasonable terms the role of AI in the dynamics of platformed sociality and education. For the time being, these are just speculations or, perhaps, aspirations. The current situation is rather different because the outcomes of AI are unreasonably framed as revelatory and superhuman, through the systematic "manufacturing of hype and promise" (Elish & Boyd, 2018, p. 58). A more accurate framing should instead emphasise their plausibility over their accuracy and, more importantly, their dependence on contingent factors: the inference strategies of choice, the structure of the environment, and the likelihood of new incoming observations.

The automation of education: The big picture

This section addresses the problem of automation, which is, of course, related to AI as it is understood here: predictive modelling and machine learning. The section, however, takes a different route – it is still indirectly connected to the "unreasonableness" argument developed so far, but it engages in a more macroeconomic and sociological analysis of the future of education as a form of work.

According to Marx, automation is an inevitable development of capitalism – the process by which living labour becomes abstracted and assimilated within the technological process, displacing workers rather than enhancing their productivity (Marx, 2005). Marx was very critical of the utopian view of automation as an example of technology "leaping to the aid of the individual worker" (p. 702). For him, automation does not enter the production process to enhance individual productivity or to support human labour, but "to reduce massively available labour power to its necessary measure. Machinery enters only where labour capacity is on hand in masses" (ibid.) For Marx, automation is driven by the need for efficiency, that is, by the capitalist' s need to reduce potential losses caused by large amounts of human variation across an abundant, and disposable, multitude of workers.

Interestingly, Marx saw this process of displacement as a precursor of the most advanced stage of socialism, as it gives workers more free time to organise collective action. This position is somewhat echoed in recent accounts of the "post-human" opportunities offered by pervasive digitisation. Donna Haraway, for instance, saw clear links between digital automation, the feminisation of work and the rise of homework economy, understood as a broad category that does not only include jobs performed in the home, but refers to a more wide-ranging restructuring of work that broadly has "the characteristics formerly ascribed to female jobs, jobs literally done only by women. Work is being redefined as both literally female and feminized, whether performed by men or women" (Haraway, 1987, p. 22). These forms of deskilled and easily exploitable work are enabled (but, of course, not directly caused) by digital automation. They are very problematic, but according to Haraway they also set the conditions for new alliances, inherently hybrid and "cybernetic", as growing multitudes of digitally connected bodies contend with similar situations.

In short, automation is a very ambivalent concept where, traditionally, social critique and a visionary rhetoric of empowerment become entangled and sometimes confused. Against this background, it could be argued that work automation under conditions of extensive platformisation involves two different scenarios. The first scenario entails the development of software or hardware systems that can augment social practices; the second scenario is based on the creation of autonomous, self-organising systems that can completely supplant humans in a particular line of work. This distinction has been captured effectively by Aaron Benanav:

> with labour-augmenting technologies, a given job category will continue to exist, but each worker in that category will be more productive. By contrast [...] no matter how much production might increase, another telephone-switchboard operator or hand-manipulator of rolled steel will never be hired.
>
> *(Benanav, 2019, p. 9)*

In his book, Benanav reports oft-cited research (Frey & Osborne, 2017) which suggested that 47% of US jobs are at high risk of automation. A prepandemic OECD study (Nedelkoska & Quintini, 2018) made a useful distinction between global jobs that are likely to become fully automated (15%), and jobs which are set to undergo significant labour-saving and task-specific automation over the next years (32%). Similar forecasts have been proposed in relation to teaching. According to a report from McKinsey Global from the same period, more than 40% of tasks performed by primary educators (most of whom are women) during a typical workday could be automated, resulting in the need to develop new skills and become more comfortable coordinating with algorithmic systems (Madgavkar et al., 2019).

The sudden explosion of generative AI in 2023 made such predictions more compelling and even tame. As I write this chapter, a vibrant and sometimes cacophonic debate is unfolding about the abrupt disappearance or transformation of entire fields of employed or self-employed work: journalism, software development, copywriting, graphic design, and so forth. In education, similar forms of generative automation are possible or just around the corner: curriculum design, instructional planning, assessment, and entirely teacherless and personalised tutoring. Despite the admittedly disruptive role that generative AI has had in a very short time, Benanav's distinction between full ("lights out", i.e., requiring no human presence so that lights can be turned off) and partial automation remains a helpful compass to navigate the controversy. To begin with, lights out automation is not a 21st-century novelty but is part of a techno-utopian imaginary, which spontaneously and periodically reoccurs. This discourse re-arises whenever "the global economy's failure to create enough jobs causes people to question its fundamental viability" (Benanav, 2019, p. 15). The traditional logic, in this argument, is reversed – it is not the unstoppable pace of innovation that fuels the automation imaginary, but the consequences of well-documented cycles of economic stagnation and under-productivity. An ideological myopia to these structural weaknesses of capitalist modes production generates the upside-down world of the automation discourse. Proponents of this discourse then search for the technological evidence that supports their view of the causes for the declining demand for labour. In making this leap, the automation theorists miss the true story of overcrowded markets and economic slowdown that actually explains the decline in labour demand (...) Technological change then acts as a secondary cause of a low labour demand, operating within the context of the first.

(Benanav, 2019, p. 38)

Following this line of reasoning, we can posit that in sectors where there is a growing demand for productivity, there will be a stronger tendency to absorb human work and little appetite for automation. Here, the labour-saving efficiencies enabled by AI are likely to materialise mostly from individual choices, adding to pre-existing bodies of practical knowledge about self-optimisation. The ready availability of generative AI as an end-user technology, only a click away or fully integrated into familiar productivity software, is part of this scenario. Concomitantly, in sectors with low productivity-growth rates there will be incentives to automate in a more "structural" and centrally coordinated fashion – not to liberate workers from the daily toil of modern life, but to manufacture conditions of under-employment as part of cost-saving strategies.

Applied to education, this argument has two consequences. First, the magnitude of the demand for teaching, understood as a form of work that combines instruction with social functions (caretaking, disciplining, and mediated socialisation into organised structures), is the first factor to consider when speculating on the future of automation in education: the higher the demand, the less automation will be viewed as a viable proposition, because societies benefit greatly from sectors that can absorb human labour. Employed humans, however inefficient or hard to govern they may be, produce healthy economies. What is left is a view of automation as cybernetic governance – a form of control that does not pursue human replacement, but standardisation, docility, and the stultification of practice. Moreover, while task automation reduces human activity in some "core" areas, it generates new trivial tasks that demand teachers to coordinate effectively with a plethora of platforms and data-based administrative systems. This has been happening for a while. According to OECD research from 2018 (Thomson & Hillman, 2019), teachers' workload is increasing in most "developed" countries. The international average (across 30 nations) was 38.8 hours a week, with many countries exceeding this average, for instance Japanese teachers clocking an average of 56 hours a week, and several English-speaking countries (the United States, Australia and England and New Zealand) sitting above 40. The average working week for Australian teachers also increased by 2.1 hours since the previous survey was conducted in 2013. The main reasons for this increase are bloated reporting requirements, having to coach students for standardised testing, and other established professional duties like planning lessons and general administration.

The key point is that such tasks are already considerably hybrid, requiring multiple human–machine interactions with institutional LMSs, edtech apps, dashboards, and databases. In other words, there is already a significant amount of task automation occurring in formal educational settings, which goes hand in hand with the growing labour demands placed on teachers. Thus, the true horizon of automation in education becomes apparent – not lights out automation, but the apprehension and control of educational practice in the name of managerial accountability. Of course, this assessment is not based on an exhaustive review of all possible forms of practice-enhancing and time-saving automations in education. It may well be that the growing sophistication of AI will lead to freedom from repetitive educational toil, but the political-economic and historical dimensions cannot be ignored. Moreover, it would be naïve and uninformed to consider automation exclusively through the lens of AI, as if thousands of more mundane tools for cognitive offloading never existed. AI compounds upon a cumulative trajectory of automation that has not led to human emancipation and relief from the structural flaws associated with employed labour in late modernity. There is no empirical or theoretical reason to believe that matters will change anytime soon.

Conclusion

Richard Sutton is one of the foremost authorities in AI. His dedicated Wikipedia page credits him as one of the founders of modern computational reinforcement learning, which refers to fully adaptive AI systems that can improve through trial-and-error interaction. In 2019, Sutton wrote a short post on his "incomplete ideas" blog (Sutton, 2019), pondering the "bitter lesson" of more than 70 years of AI research: large-scale computation is more effective than leveraging human knowledge. He was referring to two distinct paradigms of artificial intelligence: the more conservative and tame approach that relies on knowledge representations – human expertise and wisdom are modelled and built into agents – and the more aggressive (brute force) computational approach that relies on scaling through computation and big data. Sutton captures something quite important in this dynamic: the successes of AI are often tinged with bitterness, because they systematically confirm that a less refined and blunt approach is more effective than a human-centric one. This bitterness was already apparent in one

70 The unreasonable AI of platformisation

of the earliest and most well-documented battlegrounds of AI research: computer chess. Here is how Sutton recounts it:

> The methods that defeated the world champion, Kasparov, in 1997, were based on massive, deep search. At the time, this was looked upon with dismay by the majority of computer-chess researchers who had pursued methods that leveraged human understanding of the special structure of chess. When a simpler, search-based approach with special hardware and software proved vastly more effective, these human-knowledge-based chess researchers were not good losers. They said that "brute force" search may have won this time, but it was not a general strategy, and anyway it was not how people played chess. These researchers wanted methods based on human input to win and were disappointed when they did not.

The trajectory in AI research over the past 20 years – and its growing relevance in the political economy of platformisation – proved Sutton right. In domain after domain human-centric models that tried to valorise human expertise and values were outperformed by opaque deep learning approaches that could quickly mobilise parallel computational muscle (multiple processing units at the same time) and the seemingly unlimited data pool of the internet. The intoxicating promise was to do away with labour-intensive human expertise and to reframe knowledge as a discovery – the fortuitous conclusion of automated journeys into the wilderness of relational data, guided by the notion that proceeding inductively (and indeed automatically) from proxies and left-behind traces offers a more efficient and performant route to truth.

As illustrated in this chapter, this fallacy has produced a paradigm of AI steeped in unreasonableness, understood as the inability to grasp the speculative inclinations of human nature. Despite this, the seductive promise of autonomous, human-proof machine learning clearly encapsulates the immediate horizon of the platform logic in society and, it follows, in education. Indeed, we are at a point where large language models built on the premise outlined previously (deep learning benefiting from internet-extracted trace data) have reached unprecedented levels of performance, enabling AI to replicate human communicative competence and creativity. This may well be a point of no return, and the main challenge at this juncture is a political one concerned with the regulation and governance of these systems. This is what Frank Pasquale called the "second wave" of algorithmic accountability (Pasquale, 2019), which seeks to move on from the technical goal of algorithmic improvement to ask more political questions concerned with the responsible integration of these systems in society. One of such questions is whether some of these algorithms "should be used at all and – if so – who gets to govern them". In this sense, the use of strict regulatory frameworks that explicitly prohibit certain features of automated decision-making while sanctioning others is a possibility well worth exploring in the context of education.

Pasquale's "new laws of robotics", which seek to reconfigure AI as intelligence augmentation rather than replacement and obfuscation, are an excellent starting point, but it might be warranted to extend this accountability project even further, bringing to the fore its more radical implications. For instance, it may be fitting to view the very existence of these systems as the culmination of the current historical cycle of extractive capitalism – the fullest manifestation of political-economic logics that, as the 21st century gathers pace, begin to expose their intractable consequences: pervasive exploitation, environmental degradation, mass surveillance, and profound inequalities. In this sense, they are a symptom of a full-blown and years-in-the-making crisis, and their dismantling may be viewed as a political priority and a path towards other epistemologies, temporalities, and forms of truth: slower, non-anticipatory, plural, non-binary, grounded in political and historical narratives of causality rather than statistical correlations and neural activations.

References

Ananny, M., & Crawford, K. (2018). Seeing without knowing: Limitations of the transparency ideal and its application to algorithmic accountability [Article]. *New Media and Society, 20*(3), 973–989. https://doi.org/10.1177/1461444816676645

Andrejevic, M. (2020). *Automated media*. Routledge.

Arendt, H. (1998). *The Human Condition, 2nd Edition*. University of Chicago press.

Barocas, S., & Selbst, A. D. (2016). Big Data's Disparate Impact. *California law review, 104*(3 (June 2016)), 671–732. https://www.jstor.org/stable/24758720

Benanav, A. (2019). Automation and the Future of Work—1. *New Left Review, 119*, 5–38.

Bolin, G., & Andersson Schwarz, J. (2015). Heuristics of the algorithm: Big Data, user interpretation and institutional translation. *Big Data & Society, 2*(2), 2053951715608406. https://doi.org/10.1177/2053951715608406

Bostrom, N. (2014). *Superintelligence: Paths, strategies, dangers*. Oxford University Press.

Bourdieu, P., & Passeron, J.-C. (1990). *Reproduction in education, society and culture*. Sage.

Bowker, G. C., & Star, S. L. (1999). *Sorting things out: classification and its consequences*. MIT Press.

Boyd, D. (2011). White Flight in Networked Publics? How Race and Class Shaped American Teen Engagement with MySpace and Facebook. In L. Nakamura & P. A. Chow-White (Eds.), *Race After the Internet* (pp. 203–222).

Buolamwini, J., & Gebru, T. (2018). Gender shades: Intersectional accuracy disparities in commercial gender classification. Conference on fairness, accountability and transparency.

Christian, B. (2020). *The Alignment Problem: Machine Inteliigence and Human Values* Atlantic.

Crawford, K. (2021). *Atlas of AI: Power, Politics, and the Planetary Costs of Artificial Intelligence.* Yale University Press.

Datta, A., Tschantz, M. C., & Datta, A. (2014). Automated Experiments on Ad Privacy Settings: A tale of Opacity, Choice, and Discrimination. *arXiv:1408.6491.* https://doi.org/10.48550/arXiv.1408.6491.

Dewey, J. (1930). *Democracy and education: An introduction to the philosophy of education.* Macmillan.

Elish, M. C., & Boyd, D. (2018). Situating Methods in the Mmagic of Big Data and AI. *Communication monographs, 85*(1), 57–80. https://doi.org/10.1080/03637751. 2017.1375130.

Eubanks, V. (2018). *Automating Inequality: How High-Tech Tools Profile, Police, and Punish the Poor.* St. Martin's Press.

Frey, C. B., & Osborne, M. A. (2017). The future of employment: How susceptible are jobs to computerisation? *Technological forecasting and social change, 114,* 254–280. https://doi.org/10.1016/j.techfore.2016.08.019

Gillespie, T. (2014). The Relevance of Algorithms. In T. Gillespie, P. Boczkowski, & K. Foot (Eds.), *Media technologies: Essays on communication, materiality, and society* (pp. 167–194). MIT Press.

Goel, S., Rao, J. M., & Shroff, R. (2016). Personalized risk assessments in the criminal justice system. *American Economic Review, 106*(5), 119–123. https://doi.org/10.1257/aer.p20161028

Gugerty, L. (2006). Newell and Simon's logic theorist: Historical background and impact on cognitive modeling. Proceedings of the Human Factors and Ergonomics Society Annual Meeting.

Hacking, I. (1999). *The Social Construction of What?* Harvard University Press.

Haraway, D. (1987). A manifesto for cyborgs: Science, technology, and socialist feminism in the 1980s. *Australian Feminist Studies, 2*(4), 1–42. https://doi.org/10.1080/08164649.1987.9961538

Lakoff, G. (2012). Explaining embodied cognition results. *Topics in cognitive science, 4*(4), 773–785. https://doi.org/10.1111/j.1756-8765.2012.01222.x

Madgavkar, A., Manyika, J., Krishnan, M., Ellingrud, K., Yee, L., Woetzel, J., Chui, M., Hunt, V., & Balakrishnan, S. (2019). The future of women at work: transitions in the age of automation. Retrieved 15/11/2023, from https://mck.co/3SGT7FL

Marx, K. (2005). *Grundrisse: Foundations of the critique of political economy.* Penguin UK.

Massanari, A. (2017). #Gamergate and The Fappening: How Reddit's algorithm, governance, and culture support toxic technocultures. *New Media & Society, 19*(3), 329–346. https://doi.org/10.1177/1461444815608807

Minsky, M., & Papert, S. (1969). *Perceptrons.* MIT Press.

Nedelkoska, L., & Quintini, G. (2018). Automation, skills use and training. https://doi.org/10.1787/1815199X

Newell, A., & Simon, H. (1956). The logic theory machine--A complex information processing system. *IRE Transactions on information theory, 2*(3), 61–79. https://doi.org/10.1109/TIT.1956.1056797

Olah, C., Satyanarayan, A., Johnson, I., Carter, S., Schubert, L., Ye, K., & Mordvintsev, A. (2018). The Building Blocks of Interpretability. *Distill, 3*(3).

Palmer, M. (2006). Data is the New Oil. *ANA marketing maestros*. https://ana.blogs.com/maestros/2006/11/data_is_the_new.html

Pasquale, F. (2019). The Second Wave of Algorithmic Accountability *The Law and Political Economy (LPE) Project*. https://lpeblog.org/2019/11/25/the-second-wave-of-algorithmic-accountability/

Pasquale, F. (2020). *New Laws of Robotics*. Harvard University Press.

Rohs, M., & Ganz, M. (2015). MOOCs and the claim of education for all: A disillusion by empirical data. *International review of research in open and distributed learning, 16*(6), 1–19. https://doi.org/10.19173/irrodl.v16i6.2033

Satariano, A. (2020). *British Grading Debacle Shows Pitfalls of Automating Government* Retrieved 11/11/2023 from https://www.nytimes.com/2020/08/20/world/europe/uk-england-grading-algorithm.html

Stengers, I. (2011). *Thinking with Whitehead: A Free and Wild Creation of Concepts*. Harvard University Press.

Sutton, R. (2019, 12/09/2023). The Bitter Lesson *Incomplete Ideas* - www.incompleteideas.net. http://www.incompleteideas.net/IncIdeas/BitterLesson.html

Taylor, A. (2018). The automation charade. *Logic Magazine, 5*(1). https://logicmag.io/failure/the-automation-charade/

Thomson, S., & Hillman, K. (2019). The teaching and learning international survey 2018. Australian report volume 1: Teachers and school leaders as lifelong learners. https://research.acer.edu.au/talis/6

Tubaro, P., Casilli, A. A., & Coville, M. (2020). The trainer, the verifier, the imitator: Three ways in which human platform workers support artificial intelligence. *Big Data & Society, 7*(1). https://doi.org/10.1177/2053951720919776

van de Poel, I., & Sand, M. (2021). Varieties of responsibility: two problems of responsible innovation. *Synthese, 198*(19), 4769–4787. https://doi.org/10.1007/s11229-018-01951-7

Whitehead, A. N. (2020). *Whitehead's The Function of Reason*. Lindhardt og Ringhof.

Whitman, M. (2020). "We called that a behavior": The making of institutional data. *Big Data & Society, 7*(1). https://doi.org/10.1177/2053951720932200

Zhang, Q.-S., & Zhu, S.-C. (2018). Visual interpretability for deep learning: a survey. *Frontiers of Information Technology & Electronic Engineering, 19*(1), 27–39. https://doi.org/10.48550/arXiv.1802.00614

5

UNDERSTANDING PLATFORMS

Towards a social epistemology

The concept of understanding

The *Stanford Encyclopedia of Philosophy* describes understanding as a "protean concept", on account of the historical and pervasive nature of the human desire for apprehension and meaning (Grimm, 2021). Although understanding has a lot to do with knowledge, it differs in three important ways. First, understanding is related to depth of engagement, as it tends to go beyond declarative (knowing that) and procedural (knowing how) dimensions of knowledge to extend into the domains of insight and perspective, providing an ability to "see the bigger picture" and appreciate the context in which multiple forms of knowledge emerge. Second, understanding implies an ability to grasp meaning. For some, meaning is about the distinction between true and false (e.g., a statement which is meaningless because it lacks truth); for others, it is related to existential purpose (e.g., when someone argues that "life has no meaning"). There is an analytical distinction between these two interpretations, but also some overlap as experiences categorised as untrue often correlate with feelings of inauthenticity and existential emptiness. Third, understanding can be framed as a form of "epistemic success", that is, the act of reaching a superior grasp of a topic (Elgin, 2017), reflecting a holistic apprehension that surpasses mere epistemological proficiency, that is, factual accuracy and knowing one's way around a problem. As such, understanding involves more than "knowing the various truths that belong to a suitably tethered comprehensive, coherent account of the matter. The understander must also grasp how the various truths relate to each other and to other elements of the account" (ibid., p. 46). In addition, understanding

DOI: 10.4324/9781003099826-5

Understanding platforms **75**

implies the internalisation of the rules that regulate a certain practical domain, a "savoir faire" that translates in habitual and embodied competence.

In cognitive psychology, understanding is a feature that emerges from the development of schemas which can effectively steer perception and thinking. The foundational work of De Groot (2008) and Chase and Simon (1973) demonstrated that expert chess players possess a markedly superior ability compared to novices in recreating chess configurations from actual games that were only briefly observed. However, these experts do not exhibit notable differences from beginners when tasked with reproducing configurations that are randomly arranged. This occurs because arranging chess pieces randomly disrupts the ability of experienced players to identify meaningful patterns – they cannot understand what is happening on the board. Thus, what separates expert players from novices is not mere memorisation, but a subtler propensity to understand layouts and strategies at a glance. According to this cognitive perspective, understanding can be described as a state that occurs when the information in our long-term memory, stored through practice and training, permits us to quickly recognise the characteristics of a situation, giving us indications as to what to do and when to do it: we "get it".

Beyond psychology, understanding is a key problematic in epistemology, the branch of philosophy concerned with the nature of knowledge. In this context, philosophical wisdom holds that true understanding cannot be acquired only by observing a more knowledgeable other in a traditional teacher–student interaction. Understanding requires a degree of experiential investment that draws on moral and affective energies as much as cognitive functions. For the German philosopher Hans-Georg Gadamer, such experiential understanding is inextricably tied with our ability to communicate, which provides us with the means to grasp reality at a deeper level. Among all forms of communication, writing reigns supreme according to Gadamer:

> nothing is so purely the trace of the mind as writing, but nothing is so dependent on the understanding mind either. In deciphering and interpreting it, a miracle takes place: the transformation of something alien and dead into total contemporaneity and familiarity.
>
> *(Gadamer, 2004, p. 156)*

Gadamer's notion of understanding is "ontological" because it is tied to a subjective transformation through experience, much like in Heidegger who described lived experience as a "being-in-the-world" (Dasein) (Heidegger, 1977/2010), where we must come to terms with (understand) the transient nature of existence while still being able to operate as moral beings. The emphasis on writing is also interesting, as writing, alongside speech,

76 Understanding platforms

has been examined in the cultural historical tradition of developmental psychology as a conduit to concept development, higher-order thinking, and thus comprehension. Writing and speech are part of a toolkit of man-made "technologies" that emerged independently from mental functioning but ended up shaping our ability to understand, shaping our cognitive functions to such a degree that our current mental processes are profoundly intertwined with their developmental trajectory (Olson, 1996; Vygotsky, 2012).

Against this background, which draws equally on the disciplines of psychology and the philosophical field of epistemology, it becomes possible to state the following: (a) the development of understanding is entwined with the experiential dimension; and (b) communicative tools and technologies are not passive or inert but actively involved in the dynamics of understanding – they provide a model for thinking and acting. Following from this twofold premise is the question at the heart of the chapter: is platformisation changing our ability to understand? Perhaps, a straight answer is not possible or even desirable, but I do believe that education researchers and educators must take seriously the possibility of a "novel" form of knowing and understanding associated with digitisation, automation, and predictive governance.

Platformisation as episteme

Aristotle made a seminal distinction between phronesis, which refers to experiential knowledge; techne, which relates to technical competence and possesses a higher degree of generality; and, finally, episteme which is developed through analytic rationality and pursues the highest level of generality, with objective truth as the ultimate horizon. The historian of Greek culture Marcelle Detienne (Detienne & Vernant, 1991) reminded us of a fourth type of knowledge which held great significance in ancient Greek culture: metis. Metis emerges when the general rules of epistemic and technical knowledge interact with experiential phronesis, leading to even more practical and local form of understanding – a sort of "cunning" that embraces the subtleties of strategy, foresight, and intellectual prowess and is operationalised in temporally and geographically unique settings. The contrast between the generality of techne and episteme on the one side, and the situatedness of phronesis and metis on the other, is a useful framework which configures a dialectic relationship between ways of knowing. As this tension is made visible, its political underside is also exposed. Forms of knowledge based on the definition of technical principles and the pursuit of universal rules appear as codifications of complex practices and discourses. They excel at confirmatory or evaluative tasks (e.g., to prove a theorem), but struggle to capture the generative potential of knowledge "in vivo". Therefore, they tend to become instruments of power, beholden to a rationalist worldview overly concerned with organising experience according to orthodoxy and value. These forms of knowledge classify, rank, sift, and, in some cases, justify the use of disciplining measures when someone or something does not fit inside predefined categories. Conversely, forms of knowledge that valorise situated understanding are open to the possibility of social renewal because they are in tune with the diverse and "uncountable" nature of practical knowledge, grounded in history and culture.

There is much more to the philosophical and sociological study of knowledge that cannot be covered here, such as the unresolved debate between realism and relativism, that is, between a view of knowledge as a real and consequential manifestation beyond pure discourse, and a view that instead prioritises its socially constructed nature. There is no time to engage with these controversies in this chapter, but it is at least worth reiterating the argument according to which the duality between relativism and foundationalism is very much artificial (Flyvbjerg, 1998; Maton, 2013). It was Michel Foucault who, arguably more effectively than others, rejected both relativism and essentialism and chose instead to examine how regimes of truth emerged, not as pure discourses but as binding systems that shape the world in very tangible ways and, crucially, provide a template for understanding. Knowledge, for Foucault, has politics and politics have real consequences on our ability to apprehend reality. Following this logic, Foucault borrowed the term "episteme" from Aristotle but redefined it radically as a historical and sociological category: a "total set of relations that unite, at a given period, the discursive practices that give rise to epistemological figures, sciences, possibly formalized systems" (Foucault, 1970, p. 211). Another good definition of episteme, which highlights its key function in the dynamics of understanding, is as follows:

A unitary practico-cognitive structure, a regime of truth or general politics of truth, which provides the unconscious codes and rules or holistic conceptual frameworks that define problematics and their potential resolutions and constitute views of the world comprising the most fundamental of identificatory and explanatory notions, such as the nature of causality in a given range of phenomena.

(Prado, 2018, p. 26)

Here is an example: according to Foucault, a crucial epistemological upheaval occurred in the 15th and 16th centuries, when language began to lose its direct correspondence with reality following the decline of "resemblance" as the organising principle of knowledge. Up to that point, words and their referents were held together by virtue of essential similitudes or, as Foucault

78 Understanding platforms

writes: "the names of things were lodged in the things they designated, just as strength is written in the body of the lion and regality in the eye of the eagle" (Foucault, 1966, p. 36). When this linear name-giving episteme unravelled after the renaissance, that is, when the seeds of modernity were sown, the relationship between signs and their signified became a matter of interpretation (exegesis). Nowhere is this more evident than in the vicissitudes of Don Quixote, used by Foucault as a literary case study to illustrate the dramatic epistemological transition that occurred after the Renaissance. Indeed, Foucault described Don Quixote as a "negative of the Renaissance world" (p. 47) – one of the first literary figures embodying our modern and even post-modern epistemological confusions, where "words wander off on their own, without consent, without resemblance to fill their emptiness" (ibid.). In the classic tale, Don Quixote is duty bound by the rules of heroic chivalry which, however, have broken their bonds of resemblance with reality. His famously delusional adventures can be read as a form of existential breakdown, but also as a semiotic one, because the legible signs of the narrative he abides to no longer resemble the visible world he inhabits.

This rupture engenders tragedy, as Don Quixote relentlessly needs to refer to his idealised chivalric romances to confirm the possibility of his very existence: "he must endow with reality the signs-without-content of the narrative" (ibid.). What animates Don Quixote's adventures is therefore a form of exegetic labour – a constant and tireless "deciphering of the world (...) a diligent search over the entire surface of the earth for the forms that will prove that what the books say is true" (ibid.). This is tragic because that connection is lost forever and cannot be rebuilt – resemblances are now untenable and Don Quixote's efforts are forever doomed. In Cervantes' tragicomedy, Foucault saw an example of how a linguistic/semiotic connotation of understanding interacts with an existential one. This, I would argue, is one of the key insights that elevate the Foucauldian episteme as a useful concept beyond a purely historical analysis.

Following the semiotic rupture of the 15th and 16th centuries, knowledge continued towards progressive relativisation, ushering in new relationships between signs and signified no longer based on resemblances but on degrees of proximity/distance, leading to formal (measurable) criteria of order and kinship. Understanding became a matter of mathematical and probabilistic approximation, which led to "mathesis" as the logical structure of knowledge. While previously understanding the world relied on retracing alignments between signs and their referents, these relationships of resemblance are now hollowed out and replaced by probabilistic relationships between variables. This is how, as Foucault put it, language "gradually drifted away from primary designations" (ibid., p. 113) and the rift between humanistic disciplines and the positive sciences widened as a side effect. This transition has an important equivalent in the economic domain, with the appearance of exploited labour in the modern political economy of capitalism. Here, argued Foucault, we can observe the emergence of an anthropology of economic transactions where true value no longer resides in commodities but in the human labour required to create them – the "time and toil, transformed, concealed, forgotten" (ibid., p. 225). Labour became the primary site of political tensions because it is through labour that the value of commodities, that is, their meaning – is created. These intuitions help us grasp the dialectic relationship between forms of knowledge, understanding, and praxis.

The key feature of Foucauldian epistemes is that they are interlinked in networks of historical determination with multiple levels of analysis: within the macroepisteme of western culture, characterised by a trajectory towards relativisation and mathesis, smaller epistemes exist which are connected to the broader system but also bear cultural (and, indeed, technological) specificities. The glue that connects levels of analysis is the idea that understanding and meaning are *always* the result of interpretative effort in the face of growing complexity and relativisation; just as political-economic value is *always* the result of human labour in the face of the unfeeling abstractions caused by capitalist modes of production. The ramifications of this syllogism are key to the argument being developed here in relation to understanding in platformed infrastructures, enabling a more nuanced epistemological perspective on the contemporary historical moment in education.

It is important to acknowledge at this point the broader theoretical scholarship outside education where this "social epistemology" of datafied platforms has been interrogated to good effect. Notable examples are Koopman's work on the "data episteme", where rationality becomes entangled with informational and surveillance technologies and the need for data precedes and follows any form of engagement with the social world, "in such a way that we become constituted, and not merely mediated, by our data" (Koopman, 2019, p. 9). Another valuable contribution is Totaro and Ninno's work on recursion as a distinctive trait of modern rationality (Totaro & Ninno, 2014), based on a logic of numerical functions that seeks to know the word through quantification, while also establishing the cultural and material conditions for the quantification: not any quantification – for example one that might reflect the complexity and variance in the world, but only quantification that ensures efficiencies and control. Such a narrow view of quantification can easily lead to a technocratic lapse, where phenomena are trivialised and deliberately misunderstood in the pursuit of their calculability.

The platformed episteme and educational understanding

The working thesis that follows from the previous section is that a "platformed episteme" is emerging and that it engenders a specific form of educational understanding. This thesis assumes that knowledge is made possible by correlating ill-defined and contextual categories like learning, motivation, and engagement with multiple signals collected at scale. The search for proxies that may or may not correlate with educational outcomes is now extending into the biological and sub-liminal spheres – facial expression, emotion detection, brain waves, the human genome and so forth. The concept of scale is central to this thesis and requires a clarification. Scale is not the same thing as size. While size can be a co-determinant in processes of comprehension (the more books I read, the more I know and understand), the same cannot be said about scale, which instead is more akin to a mechanical "articulation" where large amounts of moving parts are mobilised under highly controlled conditions, to generate standardised and machine-readable signals (Gillespie, 2020). Thus, enormous amounts of training data can be turned into a "calculus that can then act on an enormous amount of content" (ibid., p. 2).

From this critical point of view, knowledge through scale may be quantitatively superior, but it is the very antithesis of understanding. Indeed, it is an inferior epistemological form, justified through a spurious discourse of objectivity or, worse, fortuitous intuition and discovery. This critique extends to the latest development in artificial intelligence, that is, the large language models poised to become the standard communicative and cognitive interface for interacting with platformed infrastructures. While impressive in their performance, these language models rely on a stochastic engagement with training data to simulate proficiency. They excel at generative tasks but can also be biased, inaccurate, repetitive, and prone to "hallucinating": producing content which may be highly plausible but is entirely made up (Goldstein et al., 2023). Nonetheless, their approximation of intelligent behaviour represents a form of performative understanding in its own right – one which should be taken very seriously. Through it, the twin dimensions of phronesis and metis recede further into the distance, to be replaced by a view of sensemaking as performative articulation under controlled conditions, where a carefully orchestrated semblance of epistemic proficiency achieved stochastically is mistaken as evidence of a budding artificial general intelligence (AGI). Indeed, the seemingly sentient behaviour achieved by large language models has been criticised as a mere decoy – something that becomes evident when more rigorous tests to evaluate human-like intelligence are used (van Rooij et al., 2023). Luckily, however, the loss of understanding and meaning that follows from this performance is not the end of the story, because within and around every experience of meaninglessness there are opportunities for re-signification.

Indeed, we can perhaps problematise and move past the simple dichotomy that has been examined so far, that is, between a meaningful (subjectively and culturally salient) education that pursues holistic understanding, and a meaningless (soulless and quantified) one. While compelling as a humanistic narrative, this is also a simple binary that does not fully reflect the complexity of the current sociotechnical moment. As the previous section showed, the trends we are observing now are part of a long trajectory that began with the rise of mathesis in western epistemology, propelled by a discourse of objectivism that endowed quantification and instrumental rationality with an aura of truth. The historian of science Theodore Porter noted that this brand of modern objectivism emerged gradually as an alternative to the qualitative order of subjectivity: the dimension of needs, wants and beliefs, that is, what is often associated with personal meaning (Porter, 1996). As societies became more governable through rational processes of quantification and prediction, they also became harder to understand through experience and personal meaning. So far, this argument is consistent with the premise that our ability to understand has been shrinking rather than increasing, and that platformisation emerged at the culmination of this historical process.

However, it is often lost to memory that such a dimension of "hermeneutic understanding" used to be a prerogative of the elites. In other words, the sort of Heideggerian apprehension that I described earlier in the chapter was a luxury that only a few who had access to time and financial means could afford. The denial of this individualistic dimension through standardisation and instrumental rationality was informed, partly at least, by a progressive pursuit of social justice and equality – a pursuit which was extremely imperfect in execution but still laudable in principle. Indeed, this progressive objectivism informed a great deal of social reforms, including the establishment of state-funded comprehensive education in many national contexts after the Second World War. It is not a coincidence that these reforms were assisted by rapid innovations in statistical analysis applied to large social cohorts. However, things rapidly degenerated when it became clear that objective classifications could be repurposed as disciplining instruments, easily turned against the very same underprivileged groups they were supposed to serve. There are many examples of this semiotic (and, indeed, moral) shift of objectivism – a sort of "ethical retooling" driven by neoliberal ideology (Ball, 2016, p. 1054). Porter's account of the standardised test in American education offers an enduring example.

Standardised testing was a 19th-century European (French, to be precise) invention devised to assist clinical evaluations in the budding field of psychology. It was generally administered by an expert professional to one patient at a time, and its credibility depended on the degree to which it could match expert judgement. Despite these relatively humble clinical origins, the standardised test went on to become a staple of rationalistic governance at scale, popular in the military sector and eventually finding its true home in the US education system. This was, according to Porter, "a distinctively American" (209) development – something that began as a pragmatic and progressive attempt to manage a booming and diverse student population, but in doing so it leaned into the dark tendencies of American conservative individualism. Chiefly, a desire to segregate society according to arbitrary and often racist criteria, such as "feeblemindedness". Therefore, tools designed to serve egalitarian and inclusive agendas can quickly become political instruments for ideological control, and this problematic penchant is alive and well in the contemporary digital equivalents of 19th- and 20th-century quantified governance.

In sum, objectivism has always been ethically ambivalent as a framework for political action, and, in the interest of a balanced analysis, we must acknowledge that a complex relationship exists between the good, even progressive aims of objectivism and the bad social consequences that may ensue. An awareness of this relationship means that a critique of the platform logic in education cannot be predicated solely on resisting algorithmic control and automation in the name of a more humanistic and experiential form of understanding, because knowledge obtained through abstraction and predictive analysis may be ethically acceptable in many real-life scenarios. Indeed, a total rejection of algorithmic governance is hard to justify on both epistemological and ethical grounds.

Epistemologically, the development of abstract models – understood as one of the foundational principles of software development and, therefore, platformisation – is a path to understanding because it can help apprehend reality by simplifying its complexity. As the statistician George Box famously remarked in 1976: "all models are wrong, but some are useful" (Box, 1976, p. 440), which means that modelled distillations of the world have an important heuristic purpose, as long as they are not taken at face value as isomorphic representations.

Ethically, increasing educational understanding in platformed contexts may entail that certain forms of datafication are warranted in some circumstances, as they would address an unmet need for better representation, giving visibility to historically underprivileged groups. It may well be that, despite the best intentions, manipulation and oppression are where these forms of algorithmic measurement will eventually converge, because such bad outcomes are more in tune with the extractive ideology that makes the platform logic economically attractive. However, naturalising these outcomes as destiny leads us into an impasse, especially from a perspective of educational sensemaking where the possibility of several possible futures is a necessary condition for personal and collective understanding. The very nature of education requires an openness to embrace indeterminacy and unclear potential, and indeed the developmental – that is, future facing and diverging – implications always loom large in this field. At the multiple points where the future-facing dynamics of educational potential meet and intersect, understanding is generated, that is, the educational experience is "made sense of" through a fragile and shifting balance between structural and personal propensities. In other words, believing in education entails believing in the possibility that things might be otherwise.

Scholars in Science and Technology Studies (STS) often talk about the interpretative flexibility of sociotechnical systems, that is, the fact these systems can develop and branch out in different directions because destiny is not inscribed in their nature. This is indeed a quintessentially pedagogical view: given the appropriate nurturing conditions, the world can be bettered. Admittedly, history shows that most technologies eventually stabilise around dominant socioeconomic structures and have a problematic track record of abetting exploitation and oppression. However, alternative and even revolutionary reconfigurations are still possible, especially if we hold those structures to also be man-made, that is, amenable to change and not the reflection of an immanent natural order. With this in mind, divergent forms of signification in the context of the platform logic in education are clearly possible. However, to avoid falling prey to naïve optimism, this resignification must first be problematised as a sociotechnical phenomenon in its own right.

As the previous chapter already highlighted in relation to mainstream epistemological concerns (learning and the curriculum), modern algorithmic infrastructures have evolved to benefit from technological indeterminacy and agnosticism. The promotional discourse of plug-and-play education actively pursues this agnostic relevance in the eyes of users and administrators, by welcoming all possible pedagogical orientations and theoretical allegiances. There are constructionist LMSs, direct instruction apps, personalised learning systems, mindfulness-based apps, behaviourist classroom management software, and so on. Indeed, the entire kaleidoscope of mainstream educational theory and research, as well as gimmicks and fads, can be found in edtech marketing, with established companies and emerging start-ups constantly updating standards and interfaces to allow for the continuous extension of platform functionalities. These market actors pursue profits in education by enabling ecosystems of integrations, whereby multiple features, practices, and relations between teachers and students can be slotted in and automated, as long as they are consistent with the underlying data ontologies. The heterogeneity and flexibility of platforms ecosystems can therefore be described as "meaninglessness by design" – a void that can be filled with anything a system administrator or a tech-savvy teacher might want, and an engineered state of uncertainty and possibility where educational knowledge is deliberately decoupled from the contexts where it originated.

This decoupling is certainly problematic, but the indeterminacy it engenders can perhaps be a productive condition. As some authors have noted, algorithmic architectures are particularly good at mobilising indeterminacy in culturally and politically interesting ways (Amoore, 2020; Parisi, 2019). This viewpoint suggests that the unpredictable and creative aspects of algorithms offer a unique way to re-examine structures of knowledge, opening new epistemological and ethical avenues. Such perspectives are gaining recognition in education, where some are beginning to entertain the possibility that algorithms, despite their challenges, can help break down established educational patterns, leading to "deterritorialisations of educational habit and memory" which enable progressive forms of sensemaking (Webb et al., 2019, p. 287).

Can this philosophical mobilisation of uncertainty work as a productive educational paradigm? As I write this in 2023, this is very much an open question. It will be very difficult to translate the epistemic possibilities enabled by algorithmic opacity and agnosticism into policy and practice, and while I do not dismiss the traction that these ideas are gaining in the social sciences and humanities, and conversely in some educational circles, I am more concerned with how laborious it all sounds. As context vanishes inside platformed ecosystems and the relationship between educational signs and signified becomes aleatory, more hermeneutic labour – in the "quixotic" sense described earlier – will be required, which will become increasingly taxing and stress-inducing as data are poised to inform high-stakes decisions. The platform episteme in education demands commitment and effort from non-experts and end users, who must invest personally and professionally in data infrastructures to endow machinic outputs with local and human meaning, turning them into trustworthy knowledge applicable to the educational worlds they inhabit (Perrotta et al., 2022).

This shift is particularly visible in the context of professional educational practice, where student-oriented work is becoming increasingly embroiled with data-work or AI-work: the behind-the-scenes technical toil required to establish and maintain data and semi-autonomous systems. This is the "invisible work" of information infrastructures, where contingent technical decisions become inseparable from personal sensemaking (Bowker et al., 2016). Thus, the efficiencies that these technologies promise to introduce generate a constant need for human interpretation and adaptation. Such activities may well have creative side effects, as they stimulate imagination and understanding as described earlier. On the other hand, they represent unrecognised labour upon which the entire algorithmic project relies. Educational praxis is therefore reconfigured as a project of epistemic coordination and infrastructural maintenance, superimposed onto the old regimented systems of professional practice. Under such conditions, educators must keep up with the platform logic, while simultaneously navigating managerialism, accountability, and, in many cases, a genuine commitment to relational pedagogy – which is, of course, labour-intensive in its own right.

Conclusion

This chapter argued that the current platformed episteme imposes on education the anticipatory and stochastic postulates of computational design, which configure a particular form of sensemaking that rests upon the presumed superiority of past quantitative trends over other sources of knowledge. It is not a coincidence that the language of machine learning and data science is replete with epistemological terminology: knowledge discovery, training, perception, intuition, induction, and so forth. Platformisation is undeniably a project of social (and educational) control by "superior" knowledge. It could be said that this was the case in the pre-digital era of statistical governance, but the hyper-complexity of contemporary computational capabilities has created a deeper rift between those who control the technological means of knowledge production and end users, who are reduced to sites of value extraction. Such extraction demands that people relinquish ownership over aspects of their experience in the name of convenience. The resulting efficiencies offer incentives for further engagement that capitalise on the loss of personal and social meaning: the less we own our experience within a datafied landscape, the less we understand how the underlying logic operates, and as our sensemaking ability shrinks, the "as if by magic" allure of platformisation grows. As a result, interrogating the operational aspects of digital infrastructures is not a source of knowledge but of confusion or, at best, awe. This semiotic rupture may lead to a quixotic and labour-intensive search for meaning, but also to forgoing agency altogether as an increasing number of responsibilities can be offloaded onto automated systems. Algorithmic indeterminacy, in conclusion, has a labour problem, determined largely by its operational dependency on abstracted temporalities far removed from the lives and struggles of ordinary people.

References

Amoore, L. (2020). *Cloud ethics: Algorithms and the attributes of ourselves and others*. Duke University Press.

Ball, S. J. (2016). Neoliberal education? Confronting the slouching beast. *Policy Futures in Education*, *14*(8), 1046–1059. https://doi.org/10.1177/1478210316664259

Bowker, G. C., Timmermans, S., Clarke, A., & Balka, E. (2016). Layers of silence, arenas of voice: The ecology of visible and invisible work. In *Boundary objects and beyond: Working with Leigh Star* (Vol. 8, pp. 351–373). MIT Press.

Box, G. E. (1976). Science and statistics. *Journal of the American Statistical Association*, *71*(356), 791–799. https://doi.org/10.1080/01621459.1976.10480949

Chase, W. G., & Simon, H. A. (1973). Perception in chess. *Cognitive Psychology*, *4*(1), 55–81.

De Groot, A. D. (2008). *Thought and choice in chess*. Amsterdam University Press.

Detienne, M., & Vernant, J. P. (1991). *Cunning intelligence in Greek culture and society*. University of Chicago Press.

Elgin, C. Z. (2017). *True enough*. MIT Press.

Flyvbjerg, B. (1998). Habermas and Foucault: Thinkers for civil society? *British Journal of Sociology*, 210–233. https://doi.org/10.2307/591310

Foucault, M. (1966). *The order of things*. Routledge.

Foucault, M. (1970). The archaeology of knowledge. *Social Science Information*, *9*(1), 175–185. https://doi.org/10.1177/053901847000900108

Gadamer, H.-G. (2004). *Truth and method*. Continuum.

Gillespie, T. (2020). Content moderation, AI, and the question of scale. *Big Data & Society*, *7*(2). https://doi.org/10.1177/2053951720943234

Goldstein, J. A., Sastry, G., Musser, M., DiResta, R., Gentzel, M., & Sedova, K. (2023). Generative language models and automated influence operations: Emerging threats and potential mitigations. *arXiv preprint arXiv:2301.04246*. https://doi.org/10.48550/arXiv.2301.04246

Grimm, S. (2021). *"Understanding", The Stanford Encyclopedia of Philosophy (Summer 2021 Edition)*, Edward N. Zalta (ed.). Retrieved October 22, 2023 from https://plato.stanford.edu/archives/sum2021/entries/understanding/

Heidegger, M. (1977/2010). *Basic writings: From Being and time (1927) to The task of thinking (1964)*. Routledge.

Koopman, C. (2019). *How we became our data: A genealogy of the informational person*. University of Chicago Press.

Maton, K. (2013). *Knowledge and knowers: Towards a realist sociology of education*. Routledge.

Olson, D. R. (1996). *The world on paper: The conceptual and cognitive implications of writing and reading*. Cambridge University Press.

Parisi, L. (2019). Critical computation: Digital automata and general artificial thinking. *Theory, Culture & Society*, *36*(2), 89–121. https://doi.org/10.1177/0263276418818889

Perrotta, C., Selwyn, N., & Ewin, C. (2022). Artificial intelligence and the affective labour of understanding: The intimate moderation of a language model. *New Media & Society*. https://doi.org/10.1177/14614448221075296

Porter, T. M. (1996). *Trust in numbers*. Princeton University Press.

Prado, C. G. (2018). *Starting with Foucault: An introduction to genealogy*. Routledge.

van Rooij, I., Guest, O., Adolfi, F. G., de Haan, R., Kolokolova, A., & Rich, P. (2023). Reclaiming AI as a theoretical tool for cognitive science. https://doi.org/10.31234/osf.io/4cbuv

Totaro, P., & Ninno, D. (2014). The concept of algorithm as an interpretative key of modern rationality. *Theory, Culture & Society, 31*(4), 29–49. https://doi.org/10.1177/0263276413510051

Vygotsky, L. S. (2012). *Thought and language.* MIT Press.

Webb, P. T., Sellar, S., & Gulson, K. N. (2019). Anticipating education: Governing habits, memories and policy-futures [Article]. *Learning, Media and Technology.* https://doi.org/10.1080/17439884.2020.1686015

6

SOME NOTES ON THE EMPIRICAL STUDY OF PLATFORMISATION AND AUTOMATION IN EDUCATION

Control

The notion of cybernetic feedback was first introduced by Norbert Wiener (Wiener, 1961/2019) and immediately framed, in his seminal book's very title (*Cybernetics: Or Control and Communication in the Animal and the Machine*), as a form of control regardless of whether the controlled entity is alive or not: individuals, groups, networks of machines, simple and complex organisms, financial markets, and entire social systems are fair game in the dynamics of automated cybernetic control. The underlying principle of cybernetic control is that any conceivable situation can be broken down in a series of states that range from less to more "optimal". Complex semi-autonomous systems like a biological body or a computer program can move between these states, using feedback to continuously adjust and regulate their behaviour by comparing output results with desired goals, identifying discrepancies (errors), and modifying subsequent actions to minimise these errors. This tendency to self-regulation is, to a significant extent, the result of an inherent ability – cybernetic systems (organic, machinic, individual, or composite) use internal feedback loops to align their outputs with set goals or to maintain stability amidst perturbations. However, an external control mechanism can be designed to produce stimuli that can move a system towards a desired state. This requires two steps: (a) the development of models that accurately represent the system's dynamics, behaviours, and interactions within its environment and (b) the establishment of rules and policies (algorithms) that utilise feedback from the system to effectuate control actions that guide its behaviour towards a predefined objective.

DOI: 10.4324/9781003099826-6

These automated control strategies are the cornerstone upon which platformisation is built, manifesting in algorithmic personalisation, the provision of real-time feedback, User Interface (UI) design that reflects "choice architectures" (presenting options in a particular order or form to guide decisions), the datafied administration of rewards and incentives, gamification, social proof (the strategic use of social endorsements such as likes and ratings), and so forth. Through these cybernetic techniques, platformisation nudges user engagement and attention towards a desired state (Matz et al., 2017; Thaler & Sunstein, 2021). In both social media and educational platforms, such nudges serve as subtle mechanisms to guide user behaviour towards desired outcomes. Examples include the use of notifications to inform users of new content, reminders about upcoming deadlines or assignments, and recommendations about activities and tasks based on previously completed or browsed content. In some ethically dubious instances, however, these control mechanisms target aspects considered more private or relating to an individual's ability to make autonomous choices. A troubling example of the latter scenario is the Search Engine Manipulation Effect (SEME), where search rankings are artificially altered to favour a specific candidate or no candidate at all. This manipulation has been found to subtly influence voting behaviour, with undecided voters swayed up to 20% by biased search results especially when they had no awareness of the manipulation (Epstein & Robertson, 2015). The spread of such forms of cybernetic governance over the past 25 years or so suggests that we are now living in what the French Philosopher Gilles Deleuze called "Societies of Control" (Deleuze, 2010), where technology is an instrument of modulation which operates not through the imposition of disciplinary norms but by enabling the internalisation of feedback and reward mechanisms which mobilise cognition and desire in equal measure. As Kitchin and Dodge put it: "automated management (...) enables creativity, choice and expression, at the same time it monitors, regulates, and structures. In this sense, societies of control are seductive to participants" (Kitchin & Dodge, 2011, p. 90).

Extending from this "societies of control" premise, I argue that platformisation should be examined empirically as a framework to control public life and subjectivity, coexisting and sometimes supplanting traditional approaches to democratic cohabitation. In this sense, the study of platformisation will entail, philosophically and empirically, a concern for the "embedding of techno-linguistic automated devices in the continuum of social behaviour and communication" (Berardi, 2013, p. 25), where the term "techno-linguistic automated device" refers to a broad category that includes physical infrastructures and artefacts but also protocols, standards, and habits of mind. Science and Technology Studies (STS) researchers would describe these as entities all equally involved in political negotiations. If the politics are strong enough, then facts and relations are created, and a particular version of the world is brought into being (Latour, 2005; Law & Singleton, 2005; Mol, 1999). However, the empirical analysis of these "ontological politics" cannot be a merely descriptive affair, because we cannot ignore that the sociotechnical phenomena under scrutiny are part of a distinct teleological project that aims "to make actions and enunciations predictable and manageable, and finally reducible to the overarching goal of capitalist accumulation and expansion" (Berardi, 2013, p. 25). In this sense, the empirical study of platformisation should be subsumed under a broader critical analysis of technology and society which acknowledges at the outset the enduring existence of relations of exploitation and extraction (Fuchs, 2020; Hardt & Negri, 2018).

These relations are brought into being and reproduced at the multiple points where machinic and human agency intersect. They become visible at the design level where programmers set the rules of the procedural automation that buttresses platformisation. They operate at the very heart of the computational process, like in the human computation scenarios of Amazon's Mechanical Turk (Gray & Suri, 2019), where users act in complete sync with proprietary algorithms that regulate a just-in-time job market of modular and datafied microtasks. They manifest at the point of usage, where actors draw on their cognitive energy and affect to engage productively with an automated system. Last but not least, they exist somewhere above ground where the governance criteria that regulate the emerging algorithmic landscape are established, or where investment strategies and decisions determine the material and economic conditions that make platformed ecosystems possible. As we engage in the detailed mapping of these juncture points, an entire geography begins to emerge. Navigating this geography while retaining a focus on education will require a certain technical sensibility and a willingness to engage with the modelling logic of software and data infrastructures.

Modelling

"Model" is a technical term referring to computational representations (abstractions) of concepts, processes, and systems. The driving assumption is that platformisation is made possible by modelling through computation the real world, so that it can be controlled and predicted. This process involves the use of mathematical formalisations and data to simulate the phenomenon under consideration. The list of phenomena that can be modelled runs the gamut of organised sociality and includes casual and deeply involved interpersonal relations, consumption, employment, policing, access to welfare, and, of course, multiple educational functions and activities: learning, teaching, assessment, behaviour management, and so forth. A model is developed by imposing a "grammar of action" (Agre, 1994) on a system, that is, a formalised set of symbolic representations and a computational logic for processing those representations. In plain language, this grammar of action is designed to operate as a structure that guides agency. Manovich effectively described this structure/agency dynamic at the dawn of the platform age, in a way that still rings relevant: "as we work with software and use the operations embedded in it, these operations become part of how we understand ourselves, others, and the world. Strategies of working with computer data become our general cognitive strategies" (Manovich, 2002, p. 118). The purpose of engaging critically with modelling is not to question the epistemological legitimacy of abstraction (see Chapter 5), but to highlight how abstraction quickly becomes political and aligned with computation-friendly principles – utility, efficiency, and productivity – that embody a partial vision of how societies (and, by extension, education) should be governed. The empirical analysis of modelling as the key principle of platformisation is productive because it opens an interpretative window onto this political alignment. As we attempt such interpretative work, a degree of technical auditing and an appreciation for the nuances and contradictions of algorithmic design as a cultural practice can be of great assistance (Mackenzie, 2015, 2017; Seaver, 2017).

Another angle on the same premise is data infrastructure studies, where the empirical focus is on how power is materialised and enacted through technical specifications, development tools as well as official and unofficial computational standards. As illustrated in Chapter 2, application programming interfaces (APIs) are of particular interest in this sense, for how they operate as boundary resources that modulate power relations among the main actors involved in the politics of platformisation. Such actors include corporate owners, third-party developers, regulators and legislators, and, of course, end users – all of them directly or indirectly involved in the generation, assembly, standardisation, and transformation of data which are then channelled along multiple computational processes that claim to produce readily usable guidance for more efficient and precise decision-making (Hartong & Förschler, 2019). Thus, the convolutions of algorithmic design and data infrastructuring have a socially constitutive function that conveys a mistaken aura of neutrality, while actively concealing the contestations of social life as well as the venality of the technology industry (Williamson, 2018). The key methodological take-away here is that technical auditing is useful but not the end goal, and while it will provide important insights into the often black-boxed operations of infrastructural power, its main benefit lies in providing a rationale for a more relational and political approach to research. Having peered inside the black box with a degree of systematicity and technical awareness, we can

92 The empirical study of platformisation and automation

shift our gaze to what happens around it: the sociological and cultural meanings that animate datasets, models, APIs and other digital materialisations; the economic interests of the prediction and automation industry; the disciplinary and professional entanglements of data and computer sciences as domains where, despite objectivist aspirations being asserted in their very nomenclature, uncertainties abound and, as such, constitute valuable empirical material.

The empirical tractability of these uncertainties can be further explained by referring to Mackenzie's notion of the secondary agency of software (Mackenzie, 2006), according to which computer science may possess an allure of precision but is ultimately beholden to the vagaries of human practice. As such, it is notoriously error-prone and sensitive to multiple environmental factors and dependencies, so that changes in one part of the code or in the ecosystem that surrounds the code will introduce unexpected behaviours or cause downright failures. Thus, when algorithms become embedded in platforms and digital infrastructures, a critical observer needs only wait patiently for the inevitable breakout of their secondary agency, that is, the social and cultural factors that become visible when systems do not perform as intended. As secondary agency unfolds and, in some cases, spirals out of control, the uncertainties, disagreements, affective dispositions, and ideological leanings which used to be submerged bubble up to the surface. The advent of hyper-complex AIs such as language models, which seem to operate autonomously and can modify their behaviour in real time, may be viewed as a challenge to this principle. However, these models remain stubbornly brittle, with multiple instances of bias, inaccuracies, and even "hallucinations", where the system outputs nonsensical information that may look or sound plausible at first glance but falls apart under closer scrutiny. Secondary agency is still present in these scenarios, with biased and hallucinatory breakdowns highlighting the uncertain – and very human – nature of model design and its reliance on heuristic experimentation and fine-tuning. For instance, the choice of "hidden units" in a neural network – the "neurons" located between the input layer (where the model receives its input data) and the output layer (where the model produces its output) – is notoriously contingent and ad hoc. According to one of the most influential textbooks on deep learning, such uncertainty is largely unavoidable, as

> it is usually impossible to predict in advance which will work best. The design process consists of trial and error, intuiting that a kind of hidden unit may work well, and then training a network with that kind of hidden unit and evaluating its performance on a validation set.
>
> *(Goodfellow et al., 2016, p. 196)*

This reliance on trial and error is also visible in the crucial "initialisation" of models at training stage, which requires the specification of an initial point from which to begin the training. This initial point is so important that getting it wrong can easily lead to complete failure. Most initialisation strategies are based on simple and heuristic choices made in conditions of uncertainty, because there is still much that we do not know about algorithmic optimisation, especially in relation to complex methods like deep learning. This form of heuristic inferencing reflects a calculated negotiation of trade-offs based on the "ideological" hegemony of efficiency and is based upon a fundamentally utilitarian worldview: to increase benefits (performance) at minimum computational cost, whilst avoiding the paralysing effect of hyper-complexity. A qualitative and ethnographic insight in these decisional and evaluative processes (choice of hidden units, initialisation strategies, etc.) is currently missing and represents an interesting avenue of future research.

A short digression is needed at this point, as I can almost hear readers of this book, most of whom will plausibly have a HASS (Humanities and Social Sciences) background, expressing their reservations and anxiety at the notion that any meaningful examination of platformisation will require a degree of technical auditing. On the one hand, this is inevitable, especially if the impetus driving the empirical effort is critical in nature, because a modicum of technical know-how can shield a critic against the unavoidable bad-faith challenges to the epistemic legitimacy of their arguments. However, such work needs not happen in isolation and it certainly does not need retraining as a computer scientist. It should instead be framed as collaborative and distributed, where collaboration refers to interdisciplinarity (working with discipline experts), but also to a willingness and relative ability to engage with a growing body of accessible, yet critical, computer science knowledge. Indeed, our understanding of biases, harms, and black-boxing has increased dramatically over the past decade thanks to authors who raised such problems from a position of marginality and intersectional disadvantage in the technology industry (Barocas et al., 2017; Bender et al., 2021; Birhane & Prabhu, 2021).

Moreover, an appreciation for the technical side of things is most productive when coupled with a phenomenological interest in ordinary experiences and affects, observable when regular users make sense of platformisation in their daily interactions with digital systems, on their own terms and without any sort of expert insight. Following such a phenomenological principle means that

> we do not necessarily need access to the thing itself (whatever that may be) in order to perceive it. Accordingly, phenomena of all sorts – including

94 The empirical study of platformisation and automation

algorithms – can be accessed via experience and the ways in which they make people feel.

(Bucher, 2017, p. 32)

Equally valuable is a more traditional sociological focus on the political economy of modelling and infrastructuring. Benjamin Bratton's *The Stack: On Software and Sovereignty* (Bratton, 2015) has become something of a classic example of the latter approach. Bratton's main argument is that the platform is a new organising principle that informs cross-national governance, supported by a planetary infrastructure of computation that mimics the multilayered structure of software development: modular stacks that interoperate following an ordering pattern that is simultaneously vertically integrated and horizontally distributed. The result is a structure where power is concentrated in powerful nodes within clouds of relational data: "Instead of seeing all of these as a hodgepodge of different species of computing, spinning out on their own at different scales and tempos, we should see them as forming a coherent and interdependent whole" (Bratton, 2015, p. 5); a "general logic" of software modelling is thus generating novel geopolitical arrangements which risk upending democratic notions of sovereignty that developed over centuries. Replacing them is a "schema of machines" or "accidental megastructure" (ibid.) that undergirds a new order where multiple political forms fold into each other: fiefdoms, paywalled gardens, multisided markets, and authoritarianism. Bratton describes it as a messy process of debordering and overbordering which can be examined conceptually and empirically by engaging with the logics of algorithms and databases.

All told, Bratton's remarkable work suggests that a familiarity with the technical dimension can be a powerful ally in the empirical analysis of platformisation, but we must be wary of the tunnel vision scenario, which may arise when an analyst develops an unwarranted fascination for computational complexity leading them to underestimate the heterogeneity and provisionality of social life. For example, while impressive and rigorous as a scholarly endeavour, Bratton's enquiry struggles at times to appreciate that the hyper-complexity of the Stack is more like a house of cards; certainly a sprawling superstructure but also a fragile one, with power and capital concentrated in oligarchic circuits of accumulation temporarily held together for as long as they are profitable. The state-like function of these oligarchies is therefore iterative and buggy, suggesting that the pursuit of software isomorphism as a template for political governance is a double-edged sword: it may enable the sort of cybernetic control described at the beginning of the chapter, but it also sows the seeds of its own vulnerability. The 2020 pandemic showed this, when the imminent risk of institutional collapse (hospitals overwhelmed, schools shutting down) exposed the ramshackle nature of platform capitalism, that is, its inability to step in except as temporary opportunism, while, conversely, the value of human reproductive labour was rediscovered. Across strained national health systems doctors and nurses became heroes, while in education the edtech industry once more failed to deliver on its transformative promise, and although it served an important purpose as an emergency palliative, it only provided a subpar approximation of human pedagogy (Scarpellini et al., 2021). These considerations raise a crucial methodological question: how can we avoid accounts of superstructural determination that inadvertently lionise our objects of analysis, and thus limit the scope of our critique to sterile condemnation? There is no easy answer to this question, and indeed it exposes a raw nerve that runs throughout critical social research, with its historical overreliance on denouncing and unmasking "the true calculations underlying the false consciousnesses, or the true interests underlying the false calculations" (Latour, 2012, p. 42). In his "critique of social critique" Bruno Latour makes a very compelling point about the way in which social-theoretical analyses are averse to dealing with scenarios where actors are engaged in iterative and often petty micropolitics – "some small business-owner hesitatingly going after a few market shares, some conqueror trembling with fever, some poor scientist tinkering in his lab, a lowly engineer piecing together a few more or less favourable relationships of force" (p. 126) – choosing instead to see absolute and totalitarian forces of capitalist domination hovering over everything:

> In the first scenario, the actors were trembling; in the second, they are not. The actors in the first scenario could be defeated; in the second, they no longer can. In the first scenario, the actors were still quite close to the modest work of fragile and modifiable mediations; now they are purified, and they are all equally formidable.
>
> *(Latour, 2012, p. 126)*

As implied in the introduction to this chapter, I don't entirely follow Bruno Latour here in dismissing the larger forces of domination and exploitation that give individual actors strength and legitimacy. Even when trembling with confusion, a white middle-class English-speaking male data scientist with an MIT degree wields considerable power, embodying a structure of domination that contributed to place him where he is. Nonetheless, I agree that a tendency to overplay those forces makes critical analysis monotone and ineffective. A possible answer to the difficult question above is that the empirical analysis of platformisation should embrace a relational and distributed lens, which in principle would allow a researcher to observe explicit and implicit linkages as well as tensions in conditions of uncertainty. Such

96 The empirical study of platformisation and automation

analysis can highlight the semiotic and material instability of platformisation without shying away from issues of power and exploitation.

A possible practical strategy to achieve this outcome may involve an interest in "trials of explicitness"(Muniesa & Linhardt, 2011), that is, the very mundane circumstances in which explanations of what is going on become visible and thus researchable. Muniesa and Linhardt's notion of explication should not be viewed through an entirely anthropocentric lens, that is, something that only people can do, but as a more distributed epistemological process that reflects moments of "struggle and hesitation in which what is at stake within the implementation process needs being clarified" (p. 564). This orientation can be illustrated through an example relevant to the field of platformed education: personalised learning through learning analytics. As repeatedly mentioned throughout the book, personalisation is one of the foremost promises of platformisation in education. It refers to the use of data and predictive modelling to engage with students from diverse backgrounds, customising the learning experience to cater to their needs and motivations. How does one research this topic as a distributed collection of trials of explicitness? By examining how key explications emerge or fail to emerge across a number of interlinked empirical scenarios:

A) How individual platforms or digital infrastructure projects explain the generation and analysis of student data in their official communication and documentation.
B) How the disciplinary literature and related discourses (e.g., talks, interviews, and scholarly events) describe the use of individual computational methods in education: supervised, unsupervised, decision trees, neural networks, and so forth. Here, a study could consider the problematic aspects of educational data science as a form of expertise where predictive performance of algorithms is framed as an explanatory device.
C) How learning designers and programmers explain the interface between computation and the theories of learning that underpin personalisation. That is, the fact that algorithmic personalisation requires a model of human learning amenable to decomposition, operationalisation, and, ultimately, measurement. This model can be based on an explicit theoretical preference, like for "cognitive presence" or "cognitive load", or an implicit allegiance to a disciplinary consensus about how a particular type of knowledge (e.g., secondary school algebra) is acquired and demonstrated in formal school settings. The key point here is that personalisation algorithms in education never operate in a complete explicatory vacuum, even when learning theories are not explicitly acknowledged. For example, in most personalised learning systems learning is conceptualised as a binary and individualistic pursuit: a lone student either

knows something or not (there are no degrees), and their learning can only develop along a predefined, rational path of prerequisite achievements leading to expected next steps, without divergences except those allowed by design. In some cases, like the ASSISTments Intelligent Tutoring System (widely used in the United States), this "learning" explicitly reflects the pass/fail binary of high-stakes testing, which is then reinforced computationally by relying on probabilistic models that can only predict "knowledge states" according to a base-2 logic of 0 (knowledge is present) or 1 (knowledge is absent).

D) Finally, how explanations of the value of educational data are articulated at the level of political and economic governance. Here a study could investigate how institutional and commercial entities explain their need for ever larger volumes of data: large service providers like Google with but also hybrid public–private actors like networks of universities and government bodies developing education policies.

All the above "trials of explicitness" paint a rich picture of personalised learning in platforms. Taken together, they highlight the iterative and precarious nature of platformed education without, in principle at least, downplaying the problems, in particular its addiction to neoliberal logics of extraction. Crucially, though, they also require an ability to hold together different perspectives, which poses a significant challenge to traditional methodological assumptions, in particular the notion that there is a safe distance between an observer and a phenomenon of interest. This problem will be explored in depth in the next section.

Topology

There is an established tradition in qualitative research according to which the observer stands at a relative distance from the object of analysis. Such distance, which is epistemological as well as psychological, endures even when partaking in the daily life of locals and "natives" and creating thick descriptions that account for the multilayered nature of cultural practice (Geertz, 1988). Harold Garfinkel, the founding father of ethnomethodology – the study of ordinary forms of sensemaking in naturalistic conditions – subscribed to this implicit notion of analytic distance when he introduced the documentary method, based on the principle that a particular unit of analysis (a document) can be treated as a stand-in for something else, usually a broader pattern or mechanism (Garfinkel, 1996). In this regard, the distance between the observer and the object of analysis is mirrored in the distance between the document and the phenomenon of interest that lies beyond the context or activity under consideration. This view of interpretative methodology is clearly couched in colonialism and positivism and is increasingly under attack. Does an external "other" have the ethical and epistemological prerogative to observe a culture from an outside perspective? This question is particularly fraught in the context of scholarship that wishes to engage with historically oppressed peoples on their own terms, leading in some cases to the conclusion that it is hard, sometimes impossible, to say anything meaningful or authentic about a group you do not belong to.

These are important discussions in social research and to an extent they are entwined with the contradictory nature of academic work, where privileged researchers operating within the parameters of neoliberal higher education engage in interpretative, often critical, work that seeks to challenge the status quo. What transpires from these debates is a tension between the inside and the outside; a tension where inhabiting a particular condition comes with considerable strings attached that shape the nature of an empirical account by either conferring an advantageous viewpoint or, by the same token, causing a sort of myopia of the intellect. The problem does not only concern critical scholarship and related calls for the post-colonial reform of the academy. It speaks loudly to other matters and areas of research, albeit in different terms. On the one hand, the problem is not meant to be solved in the manner of a technical challenge, but acknowledged as a contradiction we need to come to terms with through reflexivity and contextual sensitivity. After all, the very possibility of research, regardless of one's philosophical and methodological preferences, depends partly on the existence of meaningful relations between contextual knowledge and more general explaining factors. Garfinkel, for example, suggested that ethnomethodology's central endeavour, the "rational accountability of practical actions and practical reasoning" (1996, p. 4), is grounded in indexicality: the notion that meaning depends on contextual anchoring; hence, words have an indexical relation with the world, referencing something else around them or beyond them that helps convey their significance. Indexicality retains its relevance for interpretative analysis, and indeed it underpins rigorous analyses of data practices in situ which contributed greatly to our understanding of platformisation in education (e.g., Selwyn & Pangrazio, 2018). However, it also raises the considerable methodological challenge of extrapolating from local contexts broader problematics that extend beyond the confines of the observer–observed ensemble. A possible response to this challenge is to embrace radical forms of situationism that reject indexicality altogether and choose to treat their objects of analysis as self-contained symbolic and "emic" phenomena fully dependent on local actors' frames of reference. However, this strategy is also problematic because it brackets external influences and runs the risk of descending into irrelevance.

The key lesson that we can draw out from these unresolved methodological debates is that platformisation cannot be easily treated as a discrete unit of analysis that exists at a distance, because we are fully immersed in the semiotic and material conditions that make it possible. It may be a truism, but it is undeniable that platformisation has enabled a historically unprecedented degree of technological penetration, through near-total datafication and the cross-national interoperability of digital infrastructures. This situation does not generate a neat landscape which can be explored and mined for meaning by objective researchers moving in from a nebulous outside. Increasingly, platformisation defines the times and spaces in which we live – the "topologies" that reflect system of relations of "emplacement" not based on pre-modern hierarchies and classifications which, in the past, determined fixed and distinct localisations (the church, the house, the farmland, the noble's mansion, etc.), but on the emergence of lattice-like relations, whereby space develops by adding elements in a dynamic fashion while preserving un underlying ordering logic. This process produced strange "heterotopias" (Foucault, 1997) where time and space fold into each other, like the modern museum which evolved from a pre-modern interest in "antiquities" grounded in the specific cultural interests of patrons, to general archives of knowledge localised in public space but extending in multiple temporal directions:

> museums and libraries are heterotopias in which time never ceases to pile up and perch on its own summit [...] the idea of accumulating everything, the idea of constituting a sort of general archive, the desire to contain all times, all ages, all forms, all tastes in one place, the idea of constituting a place of all times that is itself outside time and protected from its erosion, the project of thus organising a kind of perpetual and indefinite accumulation of time in a place that will not move – well, in fact, all of this belongs to our modernity.
>
> *(Foucault, 1997, p. 7)*

It seems only warranted to see the internet of platforms as the historical continuation of this trend, with digitisation and planetary infrastructures for instantaneous communication enabling a further extension of the emplacement logic and creating heterotopias that accelerate and multiply the overlapping temporal dimensions we first encountered in the modern museum, while supercharging its accumulative function through digitisation and virtualisation. These trends reflect a "topological rationality" (Lury et al., 2012) that destabilises "former notions of distance and discontinuity through new practices of commensuration and a spatial imagination (...) that rejects the Euclidean and topographic notions of neutral, empty spaces" (Piattoeva & Saari, 2022, p. 171). Thus, a topological sensibility can inform a sophisticated methodological proposition for researching platformisation and data infrastructures in education (Decuypere, 2021), as things that do not exist at a safe distance from a privileged (usually academic) vantage point, but as an "assemblage of practices that is, among its multiple and diverse effects, reshaping academia" (Sellar, 2015, p. 773).

The relationship between the inside and the outside should therefore be acknowledged and used as a stimulus for a reflective enquiry that engages fully and deliberately with the relations of mutual determination at play: (a) how algorithmic logics regulate the flows of discourse and practice in a platform, and thus are actively implicated in the configuration of the phenomena under analysis; and (b) how the very same platform-enabled methods that we deploy for the analysis actively intervene in those phenomena, and as such are not neutral but "interested" (Asdal, 2018; Marres, 2015). Thus, the substantive and procedural dimensions of platformisation are thoroughly entangled with the affordances of digital infrastructures: studying platformisation means "doing" platformisation as well and, in part at least, reproducing the very same communicative logics that pursue cybernetic governance and capitalist exploitation.

Conclusion

To conclude this chapter, I wish to provide four methodological principles to be treated as tactical and pragmatic guidance against the background provided thus far. I hope this might prove helpful as a general framework for the critical study of platformisation, providing a middle ground between hard indexicality, which assumes a simplistic representational relation between phenomena (some things inside the observational plane pointing to other things beyond it) and radical situatedness, where the only option is throwing up hands and resorting to never venture beyond the sphere of contingent practice and sensemaking. Thus, what is being proposed here is a form of political empiricism where the analysis of platformisation cannot be separated from the analysis of the sociotechnical conditions of possibility in which platformisation occurs.

1. Map and document emic explanations of what is going through "polymorphous engagement" (Seaver, 2018). A polymorphous engagement refers to an attitude to evidence generation that requires "interacting with informants across several dispersed sites, not just in local communities, and sometimes in virtual form; it mean[s] collecting data eclectically from a disparate array of sources in many different ways" (Gusterson, 1997, p. 116). Polymorphous engagement implies, for example, that a corpus of formal knowledge can be analysed as an ethnographic informant and a powerful context for a trial of explicitness: "something to be observed

and engaged as something alive with concepts and practices not necessarily visible through the lens of single actors" (Kelty & Landecker, 2009, p. 177). In terms of conventional educational research, this constitutes a relatively unconventional method. However, it could be argued that complex and controversial phenomena like platformisation in education can only be studied through a pragmatic, yet careful, use of multiple methods that stretch well beyond a traditional reliance on interviews and other qualitative self-report methods.

2. Develop a "technographic" sensibility that targets a "critical understanding of the mechanisms and operational logic of software" (Bucher, 2018, p. 61). As mentioned earlier in the chapter, this sensibility should be based on a collaborative and distributed effort and on a relative willingness to enlist critical computer science knowledge. In addition, it should involve a phenomenological insight into digital interfaces, which can lead to a reflective understanding of how technological mechanisms and cultural aspects embedded in the design guide users and shape their experiences. This insight can be achieved through the methodical observation and documentation of technical features, honing in on actions, interactions, and incidents associated with participants' mundane engagement with digital systems (Light et al., 2018).

3. Stay with the algorithmic trouble. Drawing on Donna Haraway's invitation to cultivate a generative, post-positivist epistemology by tracing multiple nonlinear relationships between antecedents and consequences (Haraway, 2016), Louise Amoore (Amoore, 2020) outlines an approach to algorithmic interrogation as a journey of ethical discovery, accepting that an ability to recognise and valorise unexpected – and inevitable – developments, errors, and aberrations is just as important as the upholding of function, order, and rigour.

> To attend to algorithms as generating active, partial ways of organizing worlds is to substantially challenge notions of their neutral, impartial objectivity (...) the appearance of a moment of madness is a valuable instant for an ethicopolitics of algorithms because this is a moment when algorithms give accounts of themselves. When viewed from the specific propositional arrangements of the algorithm, particular actions that might appear as errors or aberrations are in fact integral to the algorithm's form of being and intrinsic to its experimental and generative capacities. I am advocating that we think of algorithms as capable of generating unspeakable things precisely because they are geared to profit from uncertainty, or to output something that had not been spoken or anticipated.
>
> *(Amoore, 2020, p. 111)*

4. Make the familiar seem strange. The playwright and critical theorist Bertolt Brecht famously introduced the concept of "Verfremdungseffekt" (the alienation effect) in theatre as part of his concept of Epic Theatre, which aimed to provoke critical thinking and social awareness among the audience (Trigger, 1975). Brecht's plays achieve this result through unconventional narrative structures and by breaking the "fourth wall" (actors directly addressing the audience). The resulting feelings of alienation prevent the audience from being passive observers prone to escapist fantasies and, instead, encourage them to maintain an analytical perspective conducive to a critique of the status quo. There is enduring merit in this approach and some of its wisdom is applicable to the study of platformisation. It certainly speaks to the tension between the inside and outside, and between distance and proximity, that has been framed in this chapter as integral to platformisation as a topic of study. In this sense, creating a deliberate and reflective sense of epistemological distance with an object of analysis, while at the same time accepting that such distance is illusory and plays a purely heuristic function, can lead to a productive state of mind for a researcher.

References

Agre, P. E. (1994). Surveillance and capture: Two models of privacy. *The Information Society*, *10*(2), 101–127. https://doi.org/10.1080/01972243.1994.9960162

Amoore, L. (2020). *Cloud ethics: Algorithms and the attributes of ourselves and others*. Duke University Press.

Asdal, K. (2018). "Interested Methods" and "Versions of Pragmatism". *Science, Technology, & Human Values*, *43*(4), 748–755. https://doi.org/10.1177/0162243918 773446

Barocas, S., Crawford, K., Shapiro, A., & Wallach, H. (2017). The problem with bias: Allocative versus representational harms in machine learning. 9th Annual Conference of the Special Interest Group for Computing, Information and Society, Philadelphia, pa.

Bender, E. M., Gebru, T., McMillan-Major, A., & Shmitchell, S. (2021). *On the dangers of stochastic parrots: Can language models be too big?* Proceedings of the 2020 Conference on Fairness, Accountability, and Transparency; Association for Computing Machinery: New York, NY, Virtual Event - Canada.

Berardi, F. B. (2013). The mind's we: Morphogenesis and the Chaosmic Spasm. In A. De Boever & W. Neidich (Eds.), *The psychopathologies of cognitive capitalism: Part one* (pp. 7–31). Archive Books.

Birhane, A., & Prabhu, V. U. (2021). Large image datasets: A pyrrhic win for computer vision? 2021 IEEE Winter Conference on Applications of Computer Vision (WACV).

Bratton, B. H. (2015). *The stack: On software and sovereignty*. MIT Press. https://doi.org/10.7551/mitpress/9780262029575.001.0001

Bucher, T. (2017). The algorithmic imaginary: Exploring the ordinary affects of Facebook algorithms. *Information, Communication & Society*, *20*(1), 30–44. https://doi.org/10.1080/1369118X.2016.1154086

Bucher, T. (2018). *If... then: Algorithmic power and politics*. Oxford University Press.

Decuypere, M. (2021). The topologies of data practices: A methodological introduction. *Journal of New Approaches in Educational Research*, *10*(1), 67–84. https://doi.org/10.7821/naer.2021.1.650

Deleuze, G. (2010). Postscript on the Societies of Control (1992). In I. Szeman & T. Kaposy (Eds.), *Cultural theory: An anthology* (Vol. Part 2: Power, pp. 139–142). Wiley.

Epstein, R., & Robertson, R. E. (2015). The search engine manipulation effect (SEME) and its possible impact on the outcomes of elections. *Proceedings of the National Academy of Sciences*, *112*(33), E4512–E4521. https://doi.org/10.1073/pnas.1419828112

Foucault, M. (1997). Of other spaces: Utopias and heterotopias. In N. Leach (Ed.), *Rethinking architecture: A reader in cultural theory* (pp. 330–336). Routledge

Fuchs, C. (2020). *Communication and capitalism a critical theory* (Vol. 15). University of Westminster Press. http://www.jstor.org/stable/j.ctv12fw7t5

Garfinkel, H. (1996). Ethnomethodology's program. *Social Psychology Quarterly*, *59*(1), 5–21. https://doi.org/10.2307/2787116

Geertz, C. (1988). *Works and lives: The anthropologist as author*. Stanford University Press.

Goodfellow, I., Bengio, Y., & Courville, A. (2016). *Deep learning*. MIT Press.

Gray, M. L., & Suri, S. (2019). *Ghost work: How to stop Silicon Valley from building a new global underclass*. Eamon Dolan/Houghton Mifflin Harcourt.

Gusterson, H. (1997). Studying Up Revisited. *PoLAR: Political and Legal Anthropology Review*, *20*(1), 114–119. https://doi.org/10.1525/pol.1997.20.1.114

Haraway, D. J. (2016). *Staying with the trouble: Making kin in the Chthulucene*. Duke University Press.

Hardt, M., & Negri, T. (2018). The powers of the exploited and the social ontology of Praxis. *tripleC: Communication, Capitalism & Critique. Open Access Journal for a Global Sustainable Information Society*, *16*(2), 415–423. https://doi.org/10.31269/triplec.v16i2.1024

Hartong, S., & Förschler, A. (2019). Opening the black box of data-based school monitoring: Data infrastructures, flows and practices in state education agencies. *Big Data & Society*, *6*(1). https://doi.org/10.1177/2053951719853311

Kelty, C., & Landecker, H. (2009). Ten thousand journal articles later: Ethnography of "the literature" in science. *Empiria. Revista de metodología de ciencias sociales* (18), 173–192. https://doi.org/10.5944/empiria.18.2009.2004

Kitchin, R., & Dodge, M. (2011). *Code/space: Software and everyday life*. MIT Press.

Latour, B. (2005). *Reassembling the social: An introduction to actor-network-theory*. Oxford University Press.

Latour, B. (2012). *We have never been modern*. Harvard University Press.

Law, J., & Singleton, V. (2005). Object lessons. *Organization*, *12*(3), 331–355. https://doi.org/10.1177/1350508405051270

Light, B., Burgess, J., & Duguay, S. (2018). The walkthrough method: An approach to the study of apps. *New Media & Society*, *20*(3), 881–900. https://doi.org/10.1177/1461444816675438

Lury, C., Parisi, L., & Terranova, T. (2012). Introduction: The becoming topological of culture. *Theory, Culture & Society*, *29*(4–5), 3–35.

Mackenzie, A. (2006). *Cutting Code: Software and Sociality* (Vol. 30). Peter Lang.

Mackenzie, A. (2015). The production of prediction: What does machine learning want? *European Journal of Cultural Studies*, *18*(4–5), 429–445. https://doi.org/10.1177/1367549415577384

Mackenzie, A. (2017). *Machine learners: Archaeology of a data practice*. MIT Press.

Manovich, L. (2002). *The language of new media*. MIT press.

Marres, N. (2015). Why map issues? On controversy analysis as a digital method. *Science, Technology, & Human Values*, *40*(5), 655–686. https://doi.org/10.1177/0162243915574602

Matz, S. C., Kosinski, M., Nave, G., & Stillwell, D. J. (2017). Psychological targeting as an effective approach to digital mass persuasion. *Proceedings of the national academy of sciences*, *114*(48), 12714–12719. https://doi.org/10.1073/pnas.1710966114

Mol, A. (1999). Ontological Politics. A Word and Some Questions. *Sociological Review*, *47*(1_suppl), 74–89. https://doi.org/10.1111/j.1467-954X.1999.tb03483.x

Muniesa, F., & Linhardt, D. (2011). Trials of explicitness in the implementation of public management reform. *Critical Perspectives on Accounting*, *22*(6), 550–566. https://doi.org/10.1016/j.cpa.2011.06.003

Piattoeva, N., & Saari, A. (2022). Rubbing against data infrastructure (s): Methodological explorations on working with (in) the impossibility of exteriority. *Journal of Education Policy*, *37*(2), 165–185. https://doi.org/10.1080/02680939.2020.1753814

Scarpellini, F., Segre, G., Cartabia, M., Zanetti, M., Campi, R., Clavenna, A., & Bonati, M. (2021). Distance learning in Italian primary and middle school children during the COVID-19 pandemic: A national survey. *BMC public health*, *21*(1), 1035. https://doi.org/10.1186/s12889-021-11026-x

Seaver, N. (2017). Algorithms as culture: Some tactics for the ethnography of algorithmic systems. *Big Data & Society*, *4*(2), 2053951717738104. https://doi.org/10.1177/2053951717738104

Seaver, N. (2018). What Should an Anthropology of Algorithms Do? *Cultural Anthropology*, *33*(3), 375–385. https://doi.org/10.14506/ca33.3.04

Sellar, S. (2015). Data infrastructure: A review of expanding accountability systems and large-scale assessments in education. *Discourse: Studies in the Cultural Politics of Education*, *36*(5), 765–777. https://doi.org/10.1080/01596306.2014.931117

Selwyn, N., & Pangrazio, L. (2018). Doing data differently? Developing personal data tactics and strategies amongst young mobile media users. *Big Data and Society*, *5*(1). https://doi.org/10.1177/2053951718765021

Thaler, R. H., & Sunstein, C. R. (2021). *Nudge: The final edition*. Yale University Press.

Trigger, B. G. (1975). Brecht and Ethnohistory. *Ethnohistory*, 51–56. https://doi.org/10.2307/481280

Wiener, N. (1961/2019). *Cybernetics or Control and Communication in the Animal and the Machine - Reissue Of The 1961 Second Edition*. MIT press.

Williamson, B. (2018). Silicon startup schools: Technocracy, algorithmic imaginaries and venture philanthropy in corporate education reform. *Critical Studies in Education*, *59*(2), 218–236. https://doi.org/10.1080/17508487.2016.1186710

7

CONCLUSION

As the book reaches its conclusion, it seems appropriate to revisit the central question: what is plug-and-play education? The preceding chapters provided several facets of an answer, which I will rapidly summarise. Plug-and-play education is what happens when the logics of digital platforms and automation become sufficiently "hegemonic" and widespread in education. These logics are the result of three intertwined processes: the foundational work of imaginaries and promises of future value, a very real and consequential process of infrastructuring, and distinctive modes of participation.

Having described these "first principles", the book tackled head-on the thorny issue of platformed education as a potentially novel form of learning and knowledge advancement. The picture that emerged was a mixed one, with opportunities for self-regulated learning going hand in hand with the self-serving validation and reproduction of narrow forms of corporate-sponsored knowledge.

The book then examined the role of AI, understood as a key operational aspect of platformisation and increasingly involved in its educational manifestations. Here, the concept of reasonableness was framed as a key problematic, which emerges when the algorithmic logics of AI create a sort of epistemological and intellectual erasure. This erasure makes it impossible to see the world in more speculative and "hopeful" ways.

Extending this argument, the book delved into a more theoretical examination of the relationship between platformisation and understanding, framed as a central educational concern that, again, highlights problems and opportunities. The main takeaway here was that the efficiencies and augmentations of AI are not fiction – they are real, but they are only half the story.

DOI: 10.4324/9781003099826-7

106 Conclusion

The automation of cognition that is occurring within and through platforms brings with it specific stipulations, in terms of new forms of laborious sense-making that must occur to make human-machine coordination viable, while mitigating its potential harms.

The last substantive chapter returned to several conceptual knots examined previously, but viewing them through the lens of methodology, thus providing more nuance to the book's composite answer. Notions like cybernetic governance and computational modelling were framed as the observable "operationalisations" of platformed education. The implication of the methodological sensitivity advocated in this last chapter is straightforward: if we want to understand plug-and-play education in a contextually relevant way, then we must be responsive to the idiosyncratic nature of global and local politics, as well as practices and subjectivities – including our own. Indeed, the shifts and trends described in the book are not happening in the same way on the global educational stage and not even within the same national education systems. Some key distinctions and commonalities between higher education and K-12 should also be considered in this final reflection.

In global higher education, highly variable sociopolitical conditions combined with local stratification processes must be accounted for when examining the present and future of platformisation. Indeed, higher education seems locked in a state of constant turbulence – simultaneously plagued by multiple crises and set on a path to continued expansion. However, by examining region-specific data about enrolments we can detect important nuances and trends. From 2000 to 2020, Europe and Northern America witnessed a 24% increase in student numbers, yet their share of global enrolment dropped from 40% to 21%. In contrast, Central and Southern Asia experienced a remarkable 268% surge in student enrolment during the same period, growing their portion of global student representation from 13% to 21% (UNESCO, 2022). These data suggest that the global move towards a "high participation" higher education paradigm (Marginson, 2016) is proceeding very much unabated. However, this trend is accompanied by a great deal of dynamism in macroregional education systems. The traditional western distinction between selective institutions with high prestige and mass-oriented ones that pursue volumes and social presence is now being increasingly challenged, as different forms of hybridisation and conflation occur. The so-called World-Class University (WCU) model popularised by international rankings has now a powerful normative influence on the global stage. Meanwhile, non-elite and historically "vocational" universities are also pursuing higher research status, in a bid for prestige and a better position in the aforementioned rankings.

The role of Central/East Asian countries in all this is particularly interesting, as an explosive growth in the demand for tertiary education cast them in a double act: deep pools of valuable migratory resources for Western universities, and budding global players eager to develop their own elite educational provision by enthusiastically espousing the WCU model. Moreover, this is happening amid a profound epistemic crisis, with the knowledge-production purpose of tertiary education increasingly threatened by utilitarian concerns.

Against this backdrop, the 2020 pandemic served as a moment of reckoning, by highlighting profound inequalities across and within global regions, and different degrees of readiness to arrange alternative forms of educational provision. As the shock was absorbed and processed in the period that followed enforced lockdowns and border closures, institutions scrambled to deliver courses that could seamlessly fluctuate between online and face-to-face, to accommodate student needs that can now differ dramatically across domestic and international cohorts and, in the latter case, can change unpredictably. For instance, in 2023 the Chinese government issued a characteristically blunt "edict" which, from one day to another, rendered many online degrees worthless and reopened the migratory flows of Chinese students to (mostly) English-speaking countries (Cassidy, 2023). The response of many globally oriented universities to such levels of turbulence is clearly laid out and singular: institutional agility enabled by digitisation and data orchestration (OECD, 2020). In particular, the sharing of data between different layers of domestic and international education systems, and between institutions and private actors, is now viewed as key to producing detailed students-as-customers information, and to enable effective adaptation to unstable market conditions.

This is how the platformisation described in the previous chapters is taking hold of global higher education: by establishing material and symbolic "openings" for the seamless insertion of data orchestration infrastructures. Nation states, however, are unable to provide the necessary resources for this orchestration effort, and semi-public individual institutions are equally unequipped (and underfunded) to do so. The result is a massive process of "cyberdelegation" (Fourcade & Gordon, 2020), with storage and analytical functions outsourced to private cloud platforms or, to be exact, to their automated black-boxed systems. Thus, corporations expand and consolidate their market dominance in the tertiary sector by acting in a "state-like" capacity and providing essential infrastructure for the smooth commodification of higher education. The most prominent example is Amazon Web Services (AWS), which has become the dominant provider of cloud infrastructure for tertiary institutions in English-speaking countries (Fiebig et al., 2021).

Of course, tertiary education is only half the story. What about platformisation in the K-12 sector? A brief historical reflection can help here.

108 Conclusion

The trajectory of technology in many relatively comparable compulsory systems (e.g., the UK, the United States, and Australia) is long and, at times, underwhelming. It can be described as a circular motion of political steering and self-sabotage, with cycles of public and private investment accompanied by an unhelpful narrative of innovation-averse schools, unjustly accused of "failing" to accomplish unrealistic goals of social mobility and individual flourishing. These issues have been examined in several excellent – now classic – critical analyses of educational technology (e.g., Cuban, 1986), which include detailed case studies of digital transformation (or lack thereof) inspired by a contradictory and polymorphous combination of utopianism, tactical pragmatism, and commercial interest (Monahan, 2005; Selwyn et al., 2017; Sims, 2017).

While the 1980s and 1990s were a period of naïve enthusiasm and patchy adoption, K-12 edtech quite literally boomed in the 2000s, thanks to a raft of ambitious policies in all three national contexts considered here. The United States led the way with the Enhancing Education Through Technology (EETT) Program in 2002, which was part of the No Child Left Behind Act. This programme aimed to improve student academic achievement through the use of technology in schools, and provided funds to state educational agencies, which in turn provided districts and schools with grants to integrate technology into the curriculum. The UK followed suit in 2004 with the Building Schools for the Future (BSF) Programme. This was a major capital investment programme aiming to rebuild or refurbish every secondary school in England over a 15-year period. While the primary focus was on improving the school infrastructure, a significant part of the programme also involved integrating ICT facilities and resources into schools. BSF was followed by the Harnessing Technology Strategy in 2008, which set out the UK government's plans to use technology to "transform" teaching and learning. Meanwhile in Australia, the pivotal moment occurred in 2007, when the opposition Federal Labor Government, in anticipation of its future governance, decided to place education at the forefront of its priorities. This led to the establishment of the National Secondary Schools Computer Fund (NSSCF), which aimed to achieve a 1:1 computer to student ratio for all Australian students in Years 9 to 12 by 2011. This initiative marked a significant step towards integrating digital technology in Australian education.

This policy dynamism – and the resulting surge in capital investment and digital infrastructuring over nearly two decades – has created a diverse and fractured landscape of pre-tertiary platformisation. These "patchworks of platforms" (Pangrazio et al., 2023) are not entirely chaotic but operate with a degree of coordination, driven by an overarching need for integration between data environments, without which the entire "house of cards" of

K-12 platformisation would crumble. This, in many cases, entails a double movement: a local effort – often ad hoc and reactive – concerned with the security and sovereignty of multiple tools and administrative systems; and a constant interfacing with district- or state-level digital infrastructures, which require schools to provide assessment data for governance purposes, and which impose varyingly restrictive compliance frameworks to regulate the procurement of new technologies.

My work as a researcher in educational technology has frequently taken me to secondary schools, initially throughout Europe and more recently in Australia. Over the last decade, I have been involved in a variety of projects and collaborations. A particularly illuminating perspective was offered to me by a senior systems manager at a large secondary state school in Melbourne. Their insights neatly encapsulate the current situation, while simultaneously shedding light on the key role that system administrators and platform managers play in the day-to-day operations of contemporary schools:

> We look after everything from the PA system to you know, to the data centre, to student devices to software and learning apps. There are literally so many (tools and platforms) it's easy to forget about them. But how we manage those, the privacy of that data, the sovereignty of that data, the security of that data, all that stuff comes under our umbrella. And we also then integrate into the department's technologies as well. They run a program called CASES21,[1] which is the student information system that sits behind everything. So, we have a number of different bodies that we must interact with. And our job essentially is as systems integrators – we take a lot of things off the shelf, and we try and form them into the size and shape that we need for our organisation and that meets our particular needs.
>
> *(name withheld, personal communication, 17 October 2023)*

During the same discussion, the transition to a cloud-based digital infrastructure was framed by my informant as a strategic decision shaped by an overriding need for efficiencies, economies of scale, and ease-of-use. The decision turned out to be very successful, but it brought into view a three-pronged tension typical of many state-funded schools. First, there is a local drive to innovate, even in the absence of clear guidance frameworks; second, there is the compliance-focused pressure of centralised education governance; third, there are the well-known issues of platformisation in an oligopolistic game of market dominance.

> These are huge mega platforms, which we invest millions in – also in terms of resources and time. We have documents and IP in there, and we must train people in how to use them in a specific way that doesn't

transfer across platforms. If we moved to Microsoft tomorrow, we would have to retrain everyone. And so, we get vendor-lock in on these things – once we are in this locked-in realm, they can start doing whatever they like. They recently started charging for Google Services. That's bait and switch: we'll get you in for free, but if you want to keep using these services, we are going to have to charge you – how much? Pick a number, how much is a productivity suite worth for a school? I wonder if this is sustainable – are they going to provide what we need as a school, or are they going to invest in what is more likely to make them money? The only remedy to all that is some sort of open source – something that is by the people for the people.

(name withheld, personal communication, 17 October 2023)

This testimony provides an excellent snapshot of platformisation in the pretertiary context, and, with it, the argument circuits back to the same broad problem noted in relation to global higher education: a collection of external and internal pressures is pushing education into the cloud. The question that is left at this point is: is there an alternative? If it exists, this alternative must be sought at the same critical juncture of socioeconomic power and computational expertise where the current cloud paradigm originated. In this sense, it seems inevitable that we should consider the potential of "decentralisation".

During the 2010–2020 decade, the intertwined worlds of technology and finance witnessed the arc of decentralised cryptocurrencies. In the wake of the global financial crash of 2008, a new model of monetary governance emerged, part of a technological attempt to remove the "middleman" function of traditional regulatory institutions, which proved time and again unable to prevent the cycles of growth and recession (or "boom and bust") of contemporary capitalism (Nakamoto, 2008). The idea was conceptually simple but computationally complex: to redistribute the regulatory and planning power held by banks and financial institutions to the crowd, understood less as "body politic" than a distributed and dispersed network of interested individuals.

At its core, this idea relied on records of financial transactions (blocks), securely linked through cryptography (blockchain), in such a way that no single actor could have excessive control over an entire list of records (ledger). Any changes to a ledger required an algorithmic approach to consensus, where decisions could only be approved through some sort of validation. This validation could be (a) "proof of work", where participants must solve complex mathematical puzzles, using energy-intensive computational resources; (b) "proof of stake", where those with the greatest financial stake are added to a randomly selected cadre of decision-makers, which is renewed periodically; or (c) a "proof of authority", where only a group of reputable and trustworthy actors – perhaps democratically elected – can act as validators, authorising transactions and adding blocks.

The story of decentralised cryptocurrencies until 2023 – the time of writing – showed that decentralisation is a very fragile aspiration, almost impossible to achieve in networks composed of many profit-seeking atomised actors and a few "nodes" with high decisional clout. In fact, cryptocurrencies operated more like pyramid schemes than distributed and decentralised networks, with relatively few early adopters making great gains, and most users locked in a frantic chase, lured in by the promise of trickle-down effects. After the highs and lows of crypto, what remains is an awareness – perhaps a hope – that the tension between centralisation and decentralisation should be viewed as pivotal to the future of digital governance in several social arenas. After all, beyond the aggressive avarice of crypto-finance, decentralisation offered true glimpses of a more progressive alternative to platformisation, that is, to a model where excessive power is concentrated in the hands of a few monopolistic actors. The trend of cooperative agroecological farming is worthy of a brief mention in this regard. Here, blockchain provided a trusted mechanism for equity and environmental sustainability, which – in principle – would enable small farmers in developing countries to get a fair price for their produce and ensure transparency in the supply chain (Rocas-Royo, 2021). Moreover, we should remember that a model of decentralised accountability existed before the recent radical scenario of peer-to-peer distributed ledgers, and indeed even before the internet of platforms. The early internet, imperfect as it was, was based on "federated architectures" where users were allowed to go offline for extended periods of time, while remaining able to communicate with a local server, without being locked in as the entire ecosystem relied on open standards and protocols. Moving towards a cooperative scenario entails other complexities, which Nick Srnicek already noted in his influential analysis of platform capitalism, and which remain valid (Srnicek, 2017): coops are profoundly disadvantaged when operating in a context that has been engineered to reward capitalist relations of accumulation and speculation, and which struggles to contain monopolistic tendencies. In such a scenario, cooperative decentralisation remains a worthwhile aspiration, but political and collective responses are also necessary: collective oversight – perhaps even ownership – of infrastructures should be seriously considered. After all, these infrastructures are already public in their scope and in their dependency on society's commons.

A final remark

As I write this, a shift is occurring in the debate around technology and its role in society, owing to artificial intelligence and, in particular, its "generative" incarnation with its mystifying ability to replicate human communication and

112 Conclusion

creativity, having already surpassed human cognitive potential in a long list of mundane and high-stakes domains: from scheduling a work meeting to protein folding. Usually, these turning points are celebrated as disruptions that sink old paradigms while creating new economic and cultural forms. Sometimes, however, they cause anxiety, as a realisation dawns that technologies may have unintended consequences which are unclear and undesirable. This discursive shift has a lot to do with platformisation – stemming as it does from the awareness that two decades of totalising datafication have placed us on the cusp of creating artificial agents that are not "aligned" with what is good about humanity, but are instead a reflection of its most problematic, destructive, and biased inclinations.

I do not entirely subscribe to these views and, by extension, to the facile notion of the disruptive or course-altering moment. Technological progress is more uncertain and political than the champions of disruptive innovation would have us believe. It is an incessant, yet piecemeal, work of advocacy that entails a careful assembling of opportunities and public interest – a work that always foregrounds some values and ideologies at the expense of others. Through this more critical lens, the current "Oppenheimer moment" of AI may be construed as a self-indulgent and self-serving exercise in aggrandisement, where the nebulous notion of a future existential threat generates economic and social hum, while obscuring issues manifesting right now in the present: labour exploitation and discrimination in the AI industry, environmental depletion and energy consumption, and representational and allocational harms downstream, that is, when AI systems come into contact with humans, mostly, if not always, through interactions with digital platforms.

Nonetheless, I concede that there is a degree of indeterminacy to the current situation. In fact, it could even be argued that education provides a vantage point from where to contemplate such indeterminacy. For better or worse, this has always been an idiosyncratic context where to study technological change. Three decades of education technology scholarship – both critical and affirmative – have proved that it is almost impossible to identify univocal and linear patterns of transformation. Schools and universities keep moving mercurially between conservatism and progressivism, with a great deal of variation between and within institutions when it comes to "degrees of digitisation". Luckily, education's distinctive mixture of aggressive datafication, political oversight, and piecemeal and improvised local adoption makes for continuously interesting and productive critical research – not unlike what was often drawn upon in this book, and which I am confident will continue in the coming years.

As a concluding thought, it is perhaps worth returning to the transition to cloud, which epitomises platformisation in education in the current historical juncture, highlighting its problems, its promises, its real and untested affordances, and its trajectory towards progressive AI integration. This may well be a point of no return, but such a radical change in the democratic and political balance of education (and society writ large) should perhaps give us some pause. The efficiencies and automations offered by the cloud carry, after all, a hefty price tag – not only in terms of contractual obligations that tie educational institutions to monopolistic corporations, but also in terms of abdication of control over crucial pedagogical dimensions, as information and knowledge disappear inside remote servers, where algorithmic microservices automatically crawl data to produce "schemas and transformations so that you don't have to spend time hand coding data flows" (AWS, 2023, p. 17). The fact that these automated processes occur without any scrutiny or agency from schools and universities – viewed reductively as "clients" – is certainly deserving of critical attention.

Note

1 Victorian Government's Computerised Administrative System Environment for Schools (CASES 21).

References

AWS. (2023). *Storage Best Practices for Data and Analytics Applications: AWS Whitepaper*. Retrieved November 14, 2023 from https://docs.aws.amazon.com/pdfs/whitepapers/latest/building-data-lakes/building-data-lakes.pdf#transforming-data-assets

Cassidy, C. (2023). *China winds back online study ban after students left scrambling to get to Australia*. Retrieved October 26, 2023 from https://www.theguardian.com/world/2023/jan/31/china-winds-back-online-study-ban-after-students-left-scrambling-to-get-to-australia

Cuban, L. (1986). *Teachers and machines: The classroom use of technology since 1920*. Teachers College Press.

Fiebig, T., Gürses, S., Gañán, C. H., Kotkamp, E., Kuipers, F., Lindorfer, M., Prisse, M., & Sari, T. (2021). Heads in the clouds: Measuring the implications of universities migrating to public clouds. *arXiv preprint arXiv:2104.09462*. https://doi.org/10.48550/arXiv.2104.09462

Fourcade, M., & Gordon, J. (2020). Learning like a state: Statecraft in the digital age. *Journal of Law and Political Economy*, *1*(1). https://doi.org/10.5070/LP61150258

Marginson, S. (2016). The worldwide trend to high participation in higher education: Dynamics of social stratification in inclusive systems. *Higher Education*, *72*, 413–434. https://doi.org/10.1007/s10734-016-0016-x

Monahan, T. (2005). *Globalization, technological change, and public education*. Routledge.

Nakamoto, S. (2008). Bitcoin: A peer-to-peer electronic cash system. *Decentralized Business Review*. https://doi.org/10.2139/ssrn.3440802

OECD. (2020). *Digital Transformation in the Age of COVID-19: Building Resilience and Bridging Divides, Digital Economy Outlook 2020 Supplement.* https://www.oecd.org/digital/digital-economy-outlook-covid.pdf

Pangrazio, L., Selwyn, N., & Cumbo, B. (2023). A patchwork of platforms: Mapping data infrastructures in schools. *Learning, Media and Technology*, *48*(1), 65–80. https://doi.org/10.1080/17439884.2022.2035395

Rocas-Royo, M. (2021). The Blockchain That Was Not: The Case of Four Cooperative Agroecological Supermarkets. *Frontiers in Blockchain*, *4*, 624810. https://doi.org/10.3389/fbloc.2021.624810

Selwyn, N., Nemorin, S., Bulfin, S., & Johnson, N. F. (2017). *Everyday schooling in the digital age: High school, high tech?* [Book]. https://doi.org/10.4324/9781315115764

Sims, C. (2017). *Disruptive fixation.* Princeton University Press.

Srnicek, N. (2017). *Platform capitalism.* Polity.

UNESCO. (2022). Higher education global data report (Summary). A contribution to the World Higher Education Conference 18–20 May 2022. https://bit.ly/3FZvdhd

INDEX

algorithmic fabulation 24
algorithmic harms 60–64
alignment problem, the 58, 112
Amazon Web Services (AWS) 10, 12, 23, 43–44, 107, 113
Application Programming Interfaces (APIs) 7; as a form of infrastructural mediation 20–24; as objects of analysis 91
archive 2, 99
Arendt, H. 58
Artificial Intelligence: contemporary approach to 55–56; in education 9; history of 53–55; latest development in 80; opportunities of 16; social acceptance of 64; two distinct paradigms of 64
assemblage 13, 30, 100
assets 4, 6, 17–18
automated decision-making 55, 61, 71
autonomy 25; and its role in self-regulated learning 36–40

Bateson, G. 45
Baudrillard, J. 20
Benanav A. 67–68
bias 24, 59–63, 80, 92–93
Bourdieu, P. 41
Bratton, B. 94

cloud, the 9–10, 22–23, 43–44, 107–109
cybernetics 36, 88, 94–100

datafication 8–9, 13–19, 29; of knowledge 42; as warranted in some circumstances 82
decentralisation 110
decolonisation 41–42
Deleuze, G. 17, 89
Derrida, J. 2
Dewey, J. 41, 62–63

edtech landscape, the 9–10; and investment strategies 18
enshittification 27; as a form of platform decay 28
epistemology 29, 34; and the limits of algorithmic reason 59–62
ethnomethodology 97
extraction 5, 8, 18, 25, 55, 90

Foucault, M. 77, 80

Gadamer, H.G. 75
generative AI 2, 56, 67, 80
Generative Pre-Trained Transformer (GPT) 2, 56
Google Classroom 4, 22

Index

governance 5, 9, 25, 43–48, 68, 82, 89, 94

Haraway, D. 46, 66, 101
hidden curriculum 41–42
higher education 27, 44, 98, 106

infrastructural curriculum 35, 41–44
infrastructural inversion 30
infrastructure studies 7–10, 42, 91
Ingold, T. 45
interoperability 8–12, 14, 21, 43, 93

K-12 30, 107–110

labour 6, 19; and its algorithmic redefinition 21; and the political economy of automation 66–69
Latour, B. 90, 95
learning analytics 7, 9, 30; as an attempt to bridge the learning sciences and the affordances of digital platforms 38–40
Lem, S. 14–15

machine learning 54–57, 70, 85
manipulation 25, 47, 89
Marx, K. 66
metacognition 35
middleware 20–21
modelling 90
MOOCs 9, 27–29
multisided markets 4–6, 94

neoliberalism 9, 29, 47, 81
neural networks 54, 64, 92, 96
Noble, D. 16
nudging 25, 60, 89

objectivism 80, 82
OECD 67, 68, 107
ontology 8, 21, 46, 75, 90

pandemic, the 1, 67, 94, 107
participation 14; and how it is shaped by infrastructures 24–29; as stratified according to socioeconomic factors 38
participatory cultures 37
personalisation 2; as a key promise of platformisation 18, 34; as an object of analysis 96
platformed episteme, the 80–85
platformisation, a definition of 3–7; empirical study of 90; and its relationship with datafication 13–14
plug-and-play logic, the 2–3; as an imaginary of value creation in education 14–19
political economy 30, 70, 79, 94
Porter, T. 81–82

Reich, J. 27
relational pedagogy 39–40
rentiership 4, 6
responsibility 40; as a key problem in platformed education 62–64

Science and Technology Studies (STS) 3, 16, 83, 89
secondary education 3, 61
self-determination 36–39, 48
self-regulated learning 35–39; and its limits in the context of platformisation 48
software, secondary agency of 92
solutionism 16
Strauss, L. 24
surveillance 2, 4, 8, 13, 25, 29–31, 38, 46, 79
symbolic violence 41–43, 60

tertiary education 3, 107
topology 44, 97–100

understanding 3, 63, 70, 74–85

Whitehead, A.N. 58

Milton Keynes UK
Ingram Content Group UK Ltd.
UKHW031503071224
451979UK00020B/212